RAF

AIR-TO-AIR REFUELLING

A PICTORIAL HISTORY

KEITH WILSON

AMBERLEY

First published 2019

Amberley Publishing
The Hill, Stroud
Gloucestershire, GL5 4EP

www.amberley-books.com

ISBN: 978 1 4456 6604 4 (print)
ISBN: 978 1 4456 6605 1 (ebook)

British Library Cataloguing in Publication Data.
A catalogue record for this book is available from
the British Library.

Typeset in 10pt on 12.5pt Celeste.
Typesetting by Amberley Publishing.
Printed in the UK.

Contents

Introduction

Cobham's Flying Circus comes to town! By the start of the 1930s, Alan Cobham was determined to mak the public 'air-minded' and he embarked on what he called his National Aviation Day display tour of th British Isles, visiting nearly 1,000 locations between 1932 and 1935. (*Cobham plc*)

There will be few readers, if any, who are unaware of the air-to-air (AAR) refuelling capabilit possessed by many major air arms across the globe. Although the history of early AAR tria goes back to the 1920s and 1930s, when the earliest trials were used to assist in setting a numbe of flight endurance records, it was during the Cold War that the true capability of the techniqu became recognised as being an absolute military necessity.

Cobham's Flying Circus

Sir Alan Cobham was an aviation adventurer, explorer and pioneer. His involvement in man long-distance flights in the 1920s and 1930s was to influence his thinking on the need and abilit to refuel aircraft in flight. However, many in aviation will remember Sir Alan as the founder c Cobham's Flying Circus, a group of like-minded aviators who toured the UK and South Afric in the 1930s, bringing the opportunity to experience flight to an entire generation. More tha 3 million people paid to see the shows with a large number actually taking to the air.

However, Sir Alan's long-term legacy will always be his invention of the hose-and-drogu air-to-air refuelling method and the formation of Flight Refuelling Limited in 1934. Cobham air-to-air refuelling would eventually have a significant influence on military aviation, and fc very many years to come!

Initially, AAR had been seen by some in commercial aviation as a potential way of gettin long-range transport aircraft across the Atlantic in a single unrefuelled leg, thereby speeding u the carriage of all all-important mail as well as providing quicker flights for the limited numbe of passengers on board. In fact, Flight Refuelling Limited operated four Harrow tanker aircra in conjunction with the Imperial Airways fleet of 'C' Class flying-boats who were attemptin to achieve a non-stop transatlantic air mail service in 1939. Initial trials were positive but th outbreak of the Second World War got in the way of further development and trials.

Second Lieutenant Cobham became a Royal Air Force flying instructor in July 1918. (*Cobham plc*)

In 1926, Alan Cobham and his cine-cameraman B. W. Emmott set off to race the *Windsor Castle* on a round trip to Cape Town and back, with Cobham eventually beating his rival by two days. Three months after returning from South Africa, Cobham and Arthur Elliot set off for Australia on 30 June 1926; this was the flight in which Cobham's long-serving engineer would be killed in a rather freak shooting incident. The aircraft was a de Havilland DH.50 lent to Cobham by the manufacturer and the round trip was ultimately completed, with Cobham arriving back in the UK on 1 October 1926. Cobham was later awarded a knighthood for his epic flight. (*Cobham plc*)

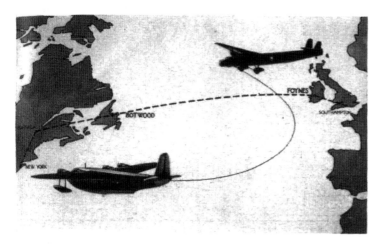

FLIGHT REFUELLING

The reliability and practicability of long distance air routes assisted by Refuelling in Flight has been proved by the Trans-Atlantic Service between Foynes and Botwood.

Refuelling makes possible greater revenue earning capacity, longer range, higher cruising speed, shorter take-off run, and better initial rate of climb. It is safe, simple and speedy.

ALL ENQUIRIES TO

FLIGHT REFUELLING LTD., FORD AERODROME, YAPTON, SUSSEX

An advertisement from 1939 showing the proposed air-to-air refuelling of the Imperial Airways 'C-class' flying boats on the first non-stop mail-carrying crossings of the Atlantic. At the time, Flight Refuelling Ltd operated four Harrow tankers, which were to be used for the refuelling task. Sixteen crossings were made (eight each way) in the late summer of 1939 before weather conditions prevented landing in Newfoundland and then the outbreak of the Second World War severely limited civil operations, bringing trials to a halt. (*Cobham plc*)

Flight Refuelling Limited's Drawing Office at Tarrant Rushton in the 1950s. (*Cobham plc*)

In May 1947, Sir Alan Cobham and ex-RAF Pathfinder Force chief Air Vice-Marshal Don Bennett began a series of air refuelled non-stop flights across the South Atlantic using converted Lancaster bombers. Sadly, it was all in vain as, although technically successful, no civil airliner has ever adopted the system for commercial use. Cobham and Bennett were photographed at Kindley Field, Bermuda, in May 1947. (*Cobham plc*)

Later, with the necessary AAR equipment available to British Forces, aircrew training commenced and a number of 'Tiger Force' Lancaster and Lincoln aircraft were converted for RAF use in the Far East. However, the operational requirement was cancelled after the advance of the American forces in the Pacific brought Japan within range of the USAAF's force of B-29 bombers; two nuclear weapons at Hiroshima and Nagasaki eventually did the rest.

USAF Solution

At the conclusion of the Second World War and as the Cold War intensified, the USA realised that it needed its long-range bombers to have the ability to strike at the heart of the Soviet Union with a sufficiently destructive bomb load. It soon realised this was not possible without the support of air-to-air refuelling assets. While some of the key Soviet targets were within the unrefuelled range of Allied bombers from bases in the UK and Anchorage, Alaska, others were well outside of their capabilities. Furthermore, there were the bombers' return journeys to be considered, as many of the Allied airfields may well have been destroyed by Soviet forces. Much of the hose and drogue equipment stockpiled for the RAF's proposed – but unused – Far East excursions were made available to the USAF for fitting to the B-29 bombers, providing both receiver and tanker aircraft.

So, while the USAF initially went down the route of Flight Refuelling Ltd's patented hose and drogue method, they would eventually opt for the purpose-designed Boeing flying boom system of AAR. Theoretically, the boom has the potential to deliver fuel at higher flow rates than a hose and drogue, although very few types of receivers (in particular, fast jets) are actually able to receive fuel at this rate. The boom also permits lower flying skills of the receiver aircraft as the boom operator inside the tanker controls the entry of the boom into the receptacle on the receiver aircraft. However, the hose and drogue method does allow for multiple receivers to refuel simultaneously on a pair of wing-mounted hose-drogue units (HDUs) while a further centreline HDU permits larger receiver types to refuel at a higher rate of transfer.

The stop-gap B-29 (and later B-50) hose and drogue solution did not last long. The USAF considered their inventory and realised the surplus piston-powered Boeing C-97A Stratocruiser would be suitable for conversion. Three were later converted, equipped with Boeing's new flying boom mounted under the rear of the fuselage, and became the KC-97A Stratotanker. Later, production variants of the tanker became the KC-97E and entered service in 1951. The final production variant of the Stratotanker was the KC-97G, which featured 700 US gallon auxiliary under-wing fuel tanks.

Unfortunately, the KC-97G proved too slow for many of the receiver aircraft – especially the fighter receivers – who were often at risk of stalling while refuelling! A possible solution was the fitting of a pair of General Electric J47 jet engines to the tanker on under-wing pylons and eighty-one aircraft were subsequently modified into the KC-97L, primarily for use by the Air National Guard units. However, the major weakness of the C-97 tanker was the fact that the aircraft needed to carry two types of fuel – Avgas to power its radial engines, as well as AVTUR to refuel the jet trade.

In April 1952, the massive eight-engine Boeing YB-52 bomber made its first flight and by 1955 it was entering service. Meanwhile, Boeing was working on the prototype four-engine jet transport the 367-80, being designed and built with both commercial airliner (as the Model 707) and military tanker roles (as the Model 717, later KC-135) in mind. An initial production order of twenty-nine KC-135A aircraft was placed in 1954 with a view to supporting the existing B-58 Hustler fleet, as well as the new B-52 Stratofortress. The KC-135A entered service in 1957. Over a period of time the number of orders for the C-135 family of aircraft eventually reached 820.

A KC-97L of the 180th Air Refuelling Squadron (ARS) of the Missouri Air Guard photographed while refuelling an A-7D Corsair II (71-314/EL) from the 23rd Tactical Fighter Wing (TFW), England AFB, Louisiana, while another (70-941/EL) awaits its turn to refuel on the Boeing flying boom. (*Wikimedia*)

Force Multiplier

In many respects, a similar need (nuclear strike capabilities during the Cold War) was responsible for the RAF's development of the single-hose Vickers Valiant and its subsequent trials. It began back in May 1951 when the prototype Vickers Type 660 Valiant made its first flight. It was designed and built in response to the Air Ministry specification B9/48.

In the same month, Colin Latimer-Needham – then Chief Engineer of Flight Refuelling Limited – produced a thorough study entitled 'Vickers B9/48 Jet Bomber Range/Bomb load Performance, unrefueled and flight-refuelled'. In the study, Latimer-Needham clearly identified the implications of the B9/48 operating in the nuclear strike role without any form of air-to-air refuelling. Basically, the range and payload ability only enabled it to reach a limited number of Soviet targets, thereby failing to achieve its Cold War strategic requirements. Latimer-Needham continued to review the aircraft's capability if air-to-air refuelling with a Lincoln, B-29 or a modified Valiant tanker were available. The results were startling! With a refuelling available on both the outward and return journey, the study demonstrated increases in range of 75 per cent, 29 per cent and 112 per cent with the respective tankers. According to the report '...flight refuelling brings within striking distance targets which would otherwise be invulnerable. Moreover, by making use of obsolete type aircraft as tankers, the bombing power of a force of B9/48 aircraft, for intermediate range operation, can be doubled or trebled.' Effectively, Latimer-Needham had seen the true 'Force Multiplier' capability of an air-to-air tanker force way back in 1951.

RAF Tanker Solution

The findings were presented to the Air Ministry, who were similarly convinced – eventually. Four types of the Vickers Valiant would enter service with the RAF: the B.1 bomber; the B(PR).1

Five Tornado GR.1 aircraft from a variety of RAF squadrons patiently fly in formation alongside a Tristar K.1 during a refuelling tow-line in AAR5, located north-east of Newcastle, on 18 December 1991. The Tornado GR.1s include ZD844/DE of No. 31 squadron, ZD745/BM of No. 14 Squadron, ZD845/AF of No. 9 Squadron, ZA461/DK of No. 31 Squadron and ZA452/BP of No. 14 Squadron. (*Keith Wilson*)

bomber or photo-reconnaissance; B(K).1 flight-refuelled receiver aircraft (bomber or tanker role) and the B(PR)K.1 flight-refuelled receiver for bomber, photo-reconnaissance or tanker roles.

Tanking Trials

Early in 1959, No. 214 Squadron, based at RAF Marham, commenced a series of operational trials of the flight-refuelling system, which went on to prove itself more than capable and provided the V-bomber force with greater flexibility and a significantly improved radius of action. Once the trials had been completed and the Valiant tanker aircraft released into service, it was capable of refuelling a variety of RAF assets. The AAR had effectively provided the UK with a true nuclear deterrent force it clearly required during the Cold War, along with a capability to refuel not just other Valiant aircraft, but a variety of other RAF assets including those involved in the Air Defence of the UK.

A crucial aspect of air-to-air refuelling during the Cold War was the UK's absolute need to defend its shores from prying Soviet aircraft. This was conducted with fighter and supporting tanker aircraft on a permanent Quick Readiness Alert (QRA), in order to respond immediately to any threats, of which there were many as the Soviet Union constantly tested the effectiveness of the QRA process. The use of tankers to support aircraft on QRA was of paramount importance, particularly when the Lightning was involved. Its spectacular performance was severely hindered by its lack of range and a supporting tanker was absolutely essential for it to successfully conduct its operations, while improving the UK's Air Defence capability.

New Tanker Aircraft

Sadly, the career of the Valiant force was cut short when, in January 1965, all aircraft were withdrawn from service following the discovery of metal fatigue within the main spars. The demise of the Valiant AAR fleet led to the introduction of the two-point Victor K.1A aircraft.

Although the Valiant was never designed to be an air-to-air refuelling tanker, following successful refuelling trials it began to enter service with No. 214 Squadron by the end of 1959. The first two aircraft converted were Valiant B(PR)K.1 aircraft WZ376 (as a tanker) and WZ390 (as a receiver), although it too was later converted to be tanker-capable. These two aircraft were photographed on 12 February 1958 while undergoing their very first air-to-air refuelling flight. (*Brooklands Museum image MP6703*)

20th TFW F-111E Aardvark 68-0077/UH, named *June Night*, photographed from the boom operator's position while receiving fuel from the flying boom on a ferry flight from Upper Heyford to Plattsburg AFB, for routine maintenance. (*Keith Wilson*)

converted from surplus B.1A bombers, which entered service in June 1965. Later, in July 1975, the three-point Victor K.2 was introduced into service. This fleet was supplemented in 1982, when six Vulcan K.2 single-point air-to-air tankers entered service as a stop-gap solution to support the Air Defence of the UK.

Later came the Hercules C.1K, the Tristar and the VC10 tanker conversions before a purpose-designed Airbus A330 MRTT (Multi-role Tanker Transport) was ordered for the RAF under a Private Finance Initiative.

Military Operations

What cannot be underestimated is the significant impact that AAR has had on military operations. Since the Korean War, all of the major conflicts across the globe have been prosecuted with the considerable assistance of air-to-air refuelling.

Without the hastily arranged modifications to Vulcan receiver aircraft the 'Black Buck' operations against the Argentinean Forces in the Falkland Island conflict would not have been possible. Without the receiver modifications rapidly completed by Marshall Aerospace on the RAF fleet of Hercules C.1 aircraft, the type's significant transport capabilities may not have been available to support British Forces on both Ascension Island and, later, the Falklands themselves.

The first Gulf War – conducted from 2 August 1990 to 28 February 1991 – demonstrated the need for absolute air superiority. This was quickly achieved over the skies of Iraq in a matter of just a few days, but would not have been possible without the significant air-to-air refuelling of most, if not all, Coalition aircraft in theatre.

On 29 June 2016, three F-35B aircraft made the journey across the Atlantic before arriving at the Royal International Air Tattoo at Fairford, in doing so making the very first public appearance of the type in the UK. Two aircraft were from the US Marine Corps while the third, an F-35B Lightning, ZM135, flown by Squadron Leader Hugh Nichols, was destined for the RAF. For the journey across the Atlantic, all three aircraft were supported by a USAF KC-10 tanker and in this image ZM137 was photographed approaching the centreline basket during one of its scheduled refuelling slots. (*Crown Copyright/Air Historical Branch image 38GpPO-20160629-080-487/SAC Tim Laurence*)

During the second Gulf War, which started in March 2003, USAF F-117 stealth aircraft were operated from their home bases in the mainland USA and were accompanied into theatre by their supporting KC-10 tanker aircraft before returning back to their home bases after delivering their ordnance.

Since then, NATO operations in Kosovo (1999), along with interventions in both Syria and Afghanistan, have all been fought with AAR as an integral and key aspect of the operations. Clearly, AAR is here to stay!

Images

As the title suggests, this is predominately a picture-led volume. In selecting the images for this book I have often been obliged to choose between quality and originality. I have gone to considerable lengths to include as many 'new' images as possible. Where a poor-quality image has been used, it is because I decided the interest value of the subject matter has warranted the decision, making it a better choice than a familiar, previously published image. After all, while the archives of the Air Historical Branch are significant, along with the other collections I have been able to 'raid', the variety of some older, historical images from specific events are somewhat limited – photography has come a long way during the history and development of air-to-air efuelling. Digital photography is having a massive impact on what is available in recent history. Nowadays, most people carry a smartphone, usually with a good-quality camera installed, so in many respects we have all become photographers, recording our history in much greater detail.

The images in this book have come from a variety of important sources. Wherever possible the source of the image has been acknowledged in the caption to each illustration. However, on occasions the widespread practice of copying images may have obscured the true origin. This may have led to some image credits in this book being incorrect. If this has occurred, it is completely unintentional and I do apologise.

From a purely personal perspective, I have been fortunate to have witnessed the skills required with RAF air-to-air refuelling operations over the last thirty years: from tow lines flown in designated AAR areas around the UK in support of local and training operations; trails to Palermo and Cyprus to position aircraft for Armament Practice Camps (APCs) at Decimomannu and Akrotiri; trails to Canada to position aircraft involved in 'Maple Flag' exercises; training exercises with Hercules tankers and receivers within the designated AAR areas off the east coast and Bristol Channel; and Tactical Air Meet exercises involving a raft of NATO aircraft participating in war games between red and blue forces off the Dutch coast. One everlasting memory from the 1992 exercise was the sight of numerous US, UK and Dutch military tanking assets flying at 2,000-foot intervals from 14,000 feet all the way up to 34,000 feet, while providing fuel for a variety of receivers including F-16s, F-111s, Tornado GR.1s and F.3s – all carefully controlled and choreographed so that receivers were able to receive fuel when required before rejoining the 'conflict'. It was like watching the proverbial 'bees around a honey pot'!

AAR has a relatively short RAF history. It was only as recently as early 1959 that No. 214 Squadron at RAF Marham commenced a series of operational trials of the hose and drogue flight-refuelling system, which proved satisfactory. In 1959 and 1960, No. 214 Squadron undertook a series of non-stop flights – many of which became unofficial distance records – demonstrating the effectiveness of the AAR system. More importantly, it provided the V-bomber force with a greater flexibility and radius of action – making them a significantly improved Nuclear Deterrent and Air Defence Force.

I have thoroughly enjoyed researching this volume, the fourth in the new 'A Pictorial History' series for Amberley Publishing. I sincerely hope this pictorial sixty-year history of RAF air-to-air refuelling enlightens and, more importantly, entertains the reader.

Keith Wilson
Ramsey, Cambridgeshire
March 2019

Acknowledgements

A project of this nature requires the help and support of many people, who have contributed in different ways to make the book possible. The author would like to offer his sincere thanks to the following:

Sebastian Cox at the Air Historical Branch, RAF Northolt, for providing the Branch's support with access to the collection of images and information, along with his encouragement and sense of humour.

My thanks must also go to Lee Barton at the Air Historical Branch for his unwavering enthusiasm, vision and attention to detail during the image selection process. Also thanks must go to his research skills, unearthing new information and responding to the never-ending stream of questions.

To Ulick McEvaddy at Omega Aerial Refuelling Services for providing images and information.

To Melissa White at Cobham plc for her extraordinary patience in answering all of the questions I posed, while also providing lots of images and information.

To Andrew Lewis at the Brooklands Museum, both for providing some excellent images while also unearthing and clearing previously classified documents relating to historic AAR milestones.

To Kieran Daly at Airbus Military, both for providing images and information.

To Terry Holloway, Alan Paul and Bridget Close at Marshalls Aerospace for providing a wealth of information and images on both the Hercules and Tristar tanker conversion programme.

To Gary Spoors, Jeff Anderson and Alan Bullen at GJD Services, Bruntingthorpe, for photographic access to the former RAF Tristar fleet held in storage at Bruntingthorpe.

To Barry Guess and Trevor Friend at BAE Systems, Farnborough, for access to the BAE Systems Heritage collection of images and information.

At Amberley Publishing I would like to thank Kevin Paul, Louis Archard and Aaron Phull for their considerable input at key stages during the book's production.

Sincere thanks are due to my sons Sam and Oliver. Thank you for your patience and support throughout the project; I couldn't have done it without you.

Finally, my special thanks must go to Carol – for being there to support me throughout the project.

The History and Development of AAR

'hen the possibility of refuelling an aircraft in the air became a reality, it was seen more as a solution for
:tending commercial operations. At the time, military applications had not really been considered but they
ould come to the fore later in proceedings! Sir Alan Cobham was the major force behind the hose-and-drogue
ethod of AAR and saw it as a way of facilitating non-stop transatlantic air mail delivery. This image shows
ie of FRL's Handley Page Harrow aircraft, appropriately registered G-AFRL, in contact with Imperial
irways' Short S30 Empire flying boat G-AFCU, named *Cabot*, over Southampton Docks in 1939. (*Cobham plc*)

Once man had mastered the art of flight, there would always be aviators who wanted to stretch the boundaries. After the First World War, the development of aircraft began to accelerate at considerable rate and there would always be those who would want to fly farther, higher and faster than the previous person. It was this 'need' that would eventually become the driving force behind the development of what we see today in the military aviation world as the 'Force Multiplier' or the 'Range Extender' – better known as 'Air-to-Air Refuelling'.

Endurance Records

The first major attempt at an endurance record occurred in the United States when two US Army Air Corps DH.4B aircraft were flown from Rockwell Field, San Diego, in April 1923. With the 'receiver' flown by Lt L. H. Smith and the 'tanker' by Lt J. P. Richter utilising a 50-foot length of refuelling hose with a trigger nozzle at its end. The observer in the receiver was able to grab the line and place the nozzle into the open filler neck of the fuel tank. It sounds rudimentary and indeed it was! However, using this method repeatedly during the attempt, the receiver was able to remain aloft for 37 hours and 15 minutes on 27/28 April. The event was publicised across the world and spurred a number of people into action, especially on this side of the Atlantic.

Late in 1927, the First Aeronautical Regiment of Belgium's Aéronautique Militaire decided to attempt to break the existing refuelling method. Using two DH.9 aircraft, Adj Aviator Louis Grooji and Sergeant Adj Groenen took to the air on 2 June and remained airborne for 60 hours 7 minutes and 30 seconds, landing on 4 June having broken the record by a significant margin.

No significant progress was made until 1929, when Major Carl Spatz with a crew of four flew a Fokker F.VII Trimotor monoplane, aptly named *The Question Mark*, for 150 hours, being supplied with fuel, oil and food by two Douglas biplanes. This achievement started a competition among commercial aviators to create a new record. It was beaten on numerous occasions but culminated in a 647½-hour flight between 21 July and 17 August 1930. The record remained until 1934, when Al and Fred Kay spent 653½ hours in a Wright-Whirlwind-powered Curtiss Robin.

Although not strictly an air-to-air refuelling record, a later attempt was made to beat the record for the longest continuous manned flight without landing in 1958 by refuelling and transferring food and supplies from a convertible-top Ford Thunderbird automobile. The attempt occurred in Las Vegas and the Cessna 172 single-engine aircraft remained aloft for 64 days, 22 hours 19 minutes and 5 seconds during a publicity flight for a Las Vegas area hotel. It only ended when the aircraft's performance had degraded to the point where the Cessna had difficulty climbing away from the refuelling car.

Cobham's Long-Distance Flights

Enter Alan Cobham into the equation. He had been a major force within pioneering aviation in the 1920s and early 1930s, and is probably best remembered for the advent of the 'National Aviation Day Displays' with the inimitable 'Cobham's Flying Circus' performing all over the UK. For many, it was probably the first occasion they had witnessed at close quarters the excitement of aviation, while also providing well over a million people with their first opportunity actually take to the air.

However, Cobham had gained great fame from a long-distance trip in 1924, when he flew Sir Sefton Brancker, Director of Civil Aviation, from the UK to India to assess landing sites for possible future air routes to Australia. The four-month trip was acclaimed as 'a triumph' by the media. Within eighteen months of the event, Cobham had organised and then carried out similar flights to South Africa and Australia. At the time, they were true pioneering events, taking place when few landing sites even existed and the DH.50 in which all of the trips were flown could only manage 120 mph. However, they did provide de Havilland with an international reputation and was crowned by a knighthood for Cobham.

However, what fascinated Sir Alan Cobham was the possibility of in-flight refuelling of commercial aircraft and in 1932 he started to take a very serious interest in the subject. He was familiar with the work of Squadron Leader (later to become Air Marshal) R. L. R. Atcherly and his 'Cross-over Contact' method of air-to-air refuelling. This involved the trailing of a horizontal line, terminating in a grapnel, from the tail of the receiver, while the tanker trailed a weighted line.

Then the tanker, by flying from side-to-side above and astern of it, enabled a contact to be made between the two lines. Once this was achieved, the refuelling hose could be passed from tanker to receiver by hauling in the receiver's line. Atcherley submitted a draft of his proposal to the Air Ministry, but it was not considered to be an improvement on existing methods. However, in March 1935, Atcherley's technique was tested with a Westland Wallace and Hawker Hart and found to be successful.

Cobham also continued experimenting with the various AAR techniques and in 1934 embarked on a non-stop flight from England to India, using an improved method for the tanker to make contact with the receiver. For the flight to India, Cobham acquired use of the Airspeed Courier G-ABXN and also obtained the backing of Lord Wakefield for the venture. The tankers were going to be a mix of Vickers Valencia and Victoria aircraft of the RAF, along with a Handley Page W.10, G-EBMR. A number of AAR trials were carried out by the Courier and W.10 before Sir Alan Cobham and his observer – Squadron Leader W. Helmore – took off from Portsmouth aerodrome on 22 September 1934 to attempt the trip. Its first refuelling rendezvous with an RAF tanker passed without incident and on the approach to Malta the Handley Page W.10 was waiting to refuel the Consul. Again, this was successful and they headed for the next refuelling point. However, after a short time, the throttle linkage on the Courier failed and the flight had to be abandoned, with Sir Alan making a wheels-up landing at Hal Far without power.

Undeterred by the incident, Sir Alan created Flight Refuelling Limited in 1934 and continued to develop the processes, with sponsorship from Imperial Airways and Shell Oil. A number of trials were also carried out on behalf of Imperial Airways and the Air Ministry. Shortly afterwards, Flight Refuelling Ltd moved to Ford Aerodrome in Sussex and took over Atcherley's work. This proved to be an excellent partnership and the method, now known as the 'looped hose' method, was developed and improved.

Transatlantic Crossings

However, the emphasis was still on commercial aviation and discussions were held on the possibility of using this new method on some of the Empire routes, as well as considering the possibility of a non-stop transatlantic crossing. This latter possibility was seen as a massive prize and work continued on making it a possibility. However, it was not until Imperial Airways acquired a pair of C-Class Empire type flying boats (named *Caledonia* and *Cambria*) in July 1937 that an attempt was made.

The *Caledonia* (G-ADHM) made her first experimental crossing from Foynes, Ireland, to Botwood, Newfoundland, on 5 July 1937. By the end of September, *Caledonia* had made six crossings and her sister *Cambria* (G-ADUV) had completed four. However, while these flights proved that the Atlantic could be crossed without refuelling, there was absolutely no payload for passengers or freight – and in particular, the mail. Experiments continued with a pick-a-back method by mounting a smaller aircraft (Short S20 G-ADHJ *Mercury*) onto the top fuselage of *Caledonia* although that initially proved unsuccessful due to the unreliable engines aboard

Mercury. However, with a change of engines the four-engine floatplane *Mercury* did make it all of the way to Canada while carrying 600 lb of mail. All of this proved the possibility of the process but clearly it would not be a profitable solution.

Around the same time, a different concept was being developed involving the refuelling of the Empire flying boat in the air. It received official agreement and was sponsored by the Director of Civil Aviation. In doing so, the project provided Sir Alan with an opportunity to demonstrate his latest AAR techniques. Once the equipment had been tested, trials began using an Armstrong Whitworth AW.23 (K3585, later G-AFRX) and the Empire flying boat *Cambria*. During January 1938, seventeen flights were carried out and all were successful.

In order to make the non-stop crossing, it was necessary to provide two bases for the tanker aircraft. The first was at Foynes, in Ireland, while the second was at Botwood in Newfoundland. Three further tankers were required to support the operation and Handley Page Harrow bomber aircraft were chosen. In early 1939, they were collected from Handley Page and given the civil registrations G-AFRG, G-AFRM and finally G-AFRL, a very convenient and appropriate one. Trials were soon carried out with what was now titled 'The Cobham Trip System' although this was later superseded when a new method of line-throwing was introduced. Subsequent trials proved the viability of the system and on 5 August 1939 the Atlantic service commenced with the Short S.30 Empire flying-boast G-AFCV leaving Southampton for the westbound trip. In all, sixteen crossings were successfully made, the crossing providing a once-weekly service. However, the service came to an abrupt end on 1 October 1939, with the outbreak of the Second World War.

The conclusion drawn from these Atlantic crossing experiments was that the system and equipment were both safe to operate and reliable for such an operation.

Pearl Harbor

Early in 1942, the bombing of the US Navy fleet at Pearl Harbor by the Japanese brought the United States into the Second World War. Flight Refuelling Limited was requested to send technical representatives to Wright Field, Ohio, to discuss with the US Army Air Force the feasibility of converting a B-17 Flying Fortress into a receiver and a B-24 Liberator into a tanker; the intention was to make a retaliatory raid on Tokyo. One set of equipment was supplied by FRL, with a view to testing and proving the system. By April 1943, the flight trials commenced at Eglin Field, Florida, and they came to a successful conclusion, the results demonstrating that the B-17 bomber's range could be increased to 5,800 miles with a full bomb load, and it was immediately followed by a planning process to make the raid happen.

Around the same time, the British Government wanted to bomb Japan but did not possess the aircraft capable of achieving the objectives, nor the bases with which to operate from. The Air Ministry decided the only way possible was to provide the Lancaster bombers with air-to-air refuelling capabilities and in early 1944 the conversion of the Lancaster aircraft into tankers and receivers would be the only practical way. These conversions were to make use of the 'looped-hose' method developed by FRL. A number of proposals were submitted for the aircraft of what was initially called 'The Long Range Force' but which was later renamed 'Tiger Force'. Fifty sets of equipment were ordered and initial prototype work was underway when major progress made by US forces in the Pacific, especially the capture of key airfields, meant that aircraft could operate from land bases. Consequently, the AAR programme for the 'Tiger Force' was cancelled.

Back to Civilian Projects

With the end of the Second World War, Sir Alan Cobham's emphasis switched back to commercial operations. Sir Alan looked at the possibility of the design and construction of an aircraft in the Brabazon 1 category. A number of proposals including the FR.10, FR.11 and FR.12 aircraft were considered, but no action was taken by either the Brabazon Committee or the commercial air transport sector.

Unfazed by this, Sir Alan started to look at the possibility of using his AAR techniques to provide a non-stop flight to Bermuda. Four specially modified Avro Lancaster aircraft were used: G-AHJU and G-AHJV, operated by British South American Airways; and two tankers, G-AHJW and G-AHJT, operated by Flight Refuelling Limited. On 28 May 1947, the first non-stop in-flight refuelled flights from London to Bermuda took place. Between 28 May and mid-August 1947, twenty-two flights (eleven in each direction) were flown.

Spurred on by the success of this route, further trials were undertaken on the London–Montreal route by the British Overseas Airways Corporation using a Consolidated LB30 Liberator II (G-AHYD) as the receiver and a fleet of four Avro Lancastrian aircraft as tankers. While no fare-paying passengers were carried during these trials, the US Government began to take a serious interest in the looped-hose method, being the only method then proving successful.

Enter the Military

In early 1948, a United Sates Army Air Force delegation visited Flight Refuelling to negotiate a contract for the air-to-air refuelling equipment for B-29 Superfortress and Boeing B-50 bombers. Initially, one B-29 was delivered to FRL's new base at Tarrant Rushton, Dorset, for conversion into a looped-hose tanker. Shortly afterwards FRL received an order for 'sufficient equipment to convert 92 KB-29M aircraft to tankers; and 74 B-29s along with 57 B-50A and B-36 aircraft into receivers'. This equipment would provide the US with the ability to carry and deliver nuclear warheads across the globe.

Shortly afterwards, the USAF requested a system that could refuel their single-seat fast jet aircraft but the looped-hose method was considered unsuitable for this application. What was required was something new and innovative.

Probe and Drogue

Driven by the need to get fuel into single-seat fast jet aircraft with the minimum of effort, Sir Alan Cobham and his team worked on a new system that would become known as the 'probe and drogue' method. Trials began in 1949 using Lancastrian G-AKDO. Later, trials were held with the A&AEE when one of their Meteor aircraft was modified as a receiver with a new nose probe which was able to plug into the drogue now trailed by the tanker aircraft. Although there were some initial teething problems, these were soon eliminated and a realistic and working solution to military air-to-air refuelling was in existence. Developments on both sides of the Atlantic were rapid, many driven by the needs of the Cold War and nuclear deterrent capabilities. The USAF followed the UK with probe and drogue and, following the conversion of some of their F-84 fighters with nose probes, underwent trails with an Avro Lincoln tanker. They also equipped one of their KB-29 aircraft into the first three-point tanker, with a pair of under-wing refuelling units complementing the third refuelling pod located in the rear fuselage. Progress with the system was rapid and developments were fast in coming. The USAF even equipped one of their

B-47 aircraft with a probe and drogue system, enabling it to refuel another B-47 in what was probably the first 'buddy-buddy' system – although the successful trial was not extended.

Flying Boom

According to the USAF, there were two perceived weaknesses with the probe and drogue system of AAR. Firstly, the rate of fuel able to be transferred was limited to a maximum of around 400 US Gallons per minute. If large aircraft were being refuelled, a much greater transfer rate was required. The second perceived weakness was the high skill level required of fast-jet receiver pilots. While RAF aircrew were trained in close formation skills during their training, perhaps USAF pilots were not? The process needed to be de-skilled or, as the US like to say, 'dumbed-down'!

Working with Boeing, the 'flying boom' seemed to offer a solution to both problems. The fuel flow rates were much higher and the boom operator in the tanker aircraft could 'fly' the boom into the receiver aircraft as long as it was able to maintain station on the tanker. Consequently, the USAF went down the flying boom route although, interestingly, neither the US Navy nor US Marine Corps did; both have preferred to remain with the probe and drogue method to this day.

RAF Cold War Bomber Support

In the late 1940s and early 1950s, the British Government had identified and ordered a range of three different V-Bomber aircraft capable of carrying and delivering the UK's own nuclear deterrent. However, as early as May 1951, Colin Latimer-Needham, the Chief Engineer of Flight Refuelling Limited, correctly identified in a study some unfortunate failings in that system. Almost two-thirds of the Soviet targets were not accessible as the range of the Valiant B.1 aircraft was insufficient to reach them. However, he also provided a solution to that problem and even identified the aircraft best suited to the required air-to-air refuelling role – a suitably modified Valiant tanker. The Air Ministry listened and authorised the required AAR trials and the rest is history.

Meanwhile, in the United States, the Cold War also spawned the massive eight-engine B-52 Stratofortress long-range bomber and, around the same time, the arrival of the Boeing 367-80, which in turn spawned the KC-135A Stratotanker equipped with the flying boom. The USAF eventually placed orders for well over 700 of them and many remain in active service today. It is expected that some will still be around in 2040 – providing the USAF with almost eighty years of tanking service!

Essential Tanking Capabilities

In the last fifty years or more, all major conflicts have been prosecuted with the considerable assistance of air-to-air refuelling – right back to the Korean War. More recently, the Falklands War demonstrated the need for AAR to allow operations to be conducted at very long distances from base. The Gulf War demonstrated the need for air superiority and this was achieved over the skies of Iraq in a matter of just a few days, but would not have been achieved without the significant air-to-air refuelling of all Allied fighter and bomber aircraft. During the second Gulf War, USAF F-117 stealth aircraft were operated from their home bases in the mainland USA and were accompanied into theatre by their supporting KC-10 tanker before returning back to the safety of their US bases.

While AAR never found a long-term place in commercial aviation, it has become an integral and essential part of just about all military operations.

In April 1923, at Rockwell Field, San Diego, Flight Lieutenants L. H. Smith and J. P. Richter took a pair of DH.4B aircraft into the air in an attempt to break the existing endurance record using a very basic in-flight refuelling system. Despite the rudimentary equipment being used, a record of 37 hours and 15 minutes was set on 27/28 April. (*Cobham plc*)

Vickers Virginia IV J7275, acting as the tanker, refuels Westland Wapati IIA K1142 using Squadron Leader Atcherley's 'cross-over' method of AAR. The RAF demonstrated this technique at the 1931 Hendon Air Pageant. (*Cobham plc*)

In 1932, Sir Alan Cobham began to take a very serious interest in the subject of air-to-air refuelling, especially in connection with record-breaking flights. In 1934, he and Bill Helmore planned a non-stop flight to India using a variety of tanker aircraft. This image of one of Aviation Displays' Handley Page W.10 aircraft, G-EBMR, refuelling Airspeed AS.5 Courier G-ABXN, was taken during trials ahead of the attempt. On 22 September 1934 they set off from Portsmouth on what was expected to be a two-day flight. Sadly, the first tanker (W.10 G-EBMM) crashed after the second refuelling and the record attempt was abandoned. (*Cobham plc*)

In 1936, the Air Ministry was persuaded to loan a pair of obsolete Vickers Virginia aircraft – a Mark VI, J7711, and a Mark X, K2668 – for trials work. After the required conversion work, the first demonstration flight was made in front of Sir Hugh Dowding (later Lord Dowding). (*Cobham plc*)

In 1943, the USAAF took an interest in Cobham's air-to-air refuelling as they needed to mount a retaliatory raid against Japan following their attack on Pearl Harbor. The trial – shown here using FRL's looped hose system – required the B-24 to fly alongside a B-17 carrying a full bomb load for 1,000 miles before transferring sufficient fuel for the B-17 to fly a total of 5,800 miles; the B-24 would then return safely to its home base. (*Cobham plc*)

Flight Refuelling Limited's two Lancaster B.3 aircraft – G-AHJWE and G-AHJU – using the looped hose refuelling system during South Atlantic trials in 1947. Sadly, G-AHJW was later lost when it crashed on 22 November 1948 while operating on the Berlin Airlift. (*Cobham plc*)

A USAF KB-29M, using FRL looped hose equipment, was photographed refuelling B-50A *Lucky Lady* during a training mission ahead of the attempt for a record round-the-world non-stop flight in March 1949. In the event, *Lucky Lady* completed the trip in a record-breaking 94 hours, being refuelled in flight four times by KB-29M tanker aircraft. (*Cobham plc*)

On 7 August 1949, in an attempt to break the existing jet aircraft endurance record, the exercise also provided publicity to the effectiveness of FRL's new hose and drogue system. Using FRL's Lancaster G-33-2 as the tanker, with Tom Marks at the controls; the company's Meteor F.3 EE397, flown by Pat Hornidge, was attempting to break the record. This image shows the Meteor refuelling over Poole Harbour. With ten refuellings taking place during the attempt, the Meteor was eventually able to remain aloft for a record-breaking 12 hours and 3 minutes. (*Cobham plc*)

Two views of the first three-point air-to-air refuelling tanker produced. In this image, the YKB-29T was photographed while simultaneously refuelling three Meteor aircraft: a pair of No. 245 Squadron F.8s (WA826 and WA829) on the electrically driven FRL Mk 11 wingtip-mounted HDUs, with FRL's Meteor Mk 4 (VZ389) refuelling from the centreline hose. (*Cobham plc*)

Just over a year after Pat Hornidge's record-breaking flight in Meteor F.3 EE997, USAF Colonels Ritchie and Schilling carried out the first non-stop crossing of the Atlantic in two Republic F-84 aircraft, with fuel provided by FRL's Lancaster and Lincoln tankers. This image shows FRL's Avro Lincoln B.2 RA657 refuelling one of the F-84 aircraft involved in the transatlantic flight. It is interesting to note that the photograph indicates the F-84 pilot has one stage of flaps deployed in order to assist him flying in close formation during the air-to-air refuelling with the much slower Lincoln. (*Cobham plc*)

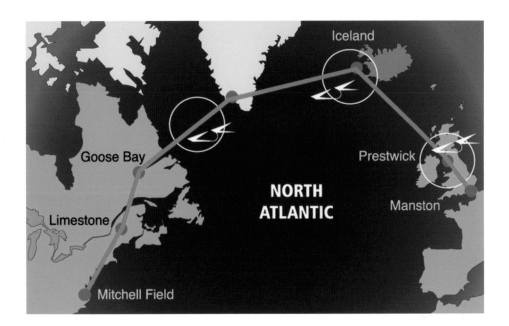

The route taken by Schilling and Ritchie is shown on this map. Though successful as a transatlantic crossing, it required three separate tanker interceptions and numerous weather reporting and rescue aircraft to be on station. Unfortunately, Ritchie was forced to eject over Goose Bay while Schilling went on to land short of his planned Washington destination, at Limestone in Maine. The refuelling points are circled on the map. (*Cobham plc*)

In the autumn of 1949, the USAF placed an order for the conversion of B-29 aircraft into receiver aircraft, one of which was specially designed to receive high flow rates of fuel, and the other a low flow rate of fuel. It also ordered a single-point tanker and another as a three-point tanker. At the same time, two Republic F-84E Thunderjet single-seat fighters were converted into receivers. This photograph was taken off the Dorset coast in 1950 and shows the single-point B-29 tanker providing fuel to one of the B-29 receivers during the refuelling trials. (*Cobham plc*)

1950, the Air Ministry ordered the conversion of sixteen Meteor F.8 aircraft into receivers. All of e aircraft to be converted were from No. 245 Squadron at RAF Horsham St Faith. After conversion, r-to-air refuelling trials were initially undertaken using FRL's Lincoln RA657, although this was er joined in the programme by SX993. This image shows one of the No. 245 Squadron Meteors, A829/A, during the refuelling trials in July 1951, probably refuelling from RA657. (*BAE Systems eritage Collection*)

1 21 July 1951, during an empted round-Britain ght, the third refuelling d been planned to take ace overhead Horsham Faith, enabling the rcraft to land with full el tanks. However, echnical problem curred with the probe ozzle valve and the ght was terminated. nce again, Lincoln A657 was the tanker d Meteor 8 WA829/A e receiver. (*BAE Systems eritage Collection image N0246*)

This image, taken during a combat mission in Korea in 1952, shows Lockheed F-80 aircraft taking on fuel from the tanker via Sargent Fletcher tip-tank probes. After making sixteen separate refuelling contacts (eight for each wing tank) in his F-80A, USAF Major Harry Dorris established a new record for turbojet aircraft of 14 hours 25 minutes while in combat conditions and in radio silence. (*Cobham plc*)

The first carrier-borne aircraft to be operated as a tanker was the North American AJ-2 Savage, photographed here refuelling a Grumman Panther. The AJ-2 Savage was fitted with a FRL A-12 HDU installed in the bomb bay. The success of this aircraft went a long way to convincing the US authorities to order the Convair R3Y-2 Tradewind flying boat tanker. (*Cobham plc*)

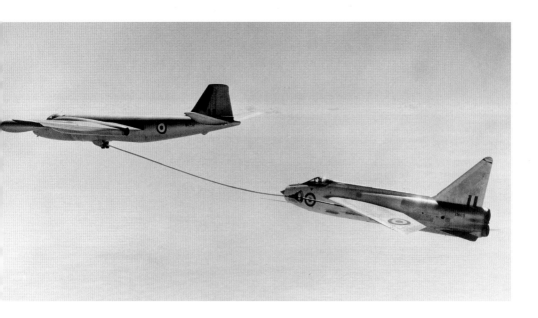

In July 1953, Canberra B.2 WH734 was delivered to Tarrant Rushton for the installation of the FRL Mk 15 HDU for high-speed and altitude trials with Valiant WZ390. In doing so, the Canberra became Britain's first jet tanker. It continued with trials work for a number of years and was photographed refuelling the first production Lightning F.1A, XM169, in late 1960. (*BAE Systems Heritage Collection*)

In September 1956, the Convair R3Y-2 Tradewind became the first aerial tanker to refuel four aircraft simultaneously. In this image, the receivers are US Navy Grumman Cougars. (*Cobham plc*)

While it had never been the intention to provide the Valiant with an in-flight refuelling capability, this eventually became perhaps the most important retrospective modification the type was to receive. The trials were conducted by a pair of Valiant B(PR)K.1 aircraft – WZ376 and WZ390 – with the former equipped with a FRL Mk 16 HDU installed into the bomb bay, while both were equipped with in-flight refuelling nose probes. This image was taken during the very first air-to-air refuelling contact, on 12 February 1958. (*Brooklands Museum image MP6704*)

Following the unexpected withdrawal of the Valiant fleet of tanker aircraft, the decision was taken to convert surplus Handley Page Victor B.1 and B.1A airframes for the air-to-air refuelling role – initially as the K.1 and K.1A respectively – each carrying a pair of FRL Mk 20B under-wing refuelling pods (HDUs) and operating as two-point tankers. Later in the conversion process – conducted by Avro at Woodford – a FRL Mk 17 refuelling pod was added within the underside of the rear fuselage, aft of the bomb bay, with the aircraft now operating as three-point tankers. XA918, part of the A&AEE's test fleet at Boscombe Down, was heavily involved in the initial trials, making its first flight after conversion to K.1 standards during the summer of 1964. In April 1965, XA918 commenced trials to obtain clearance for the centreline refuelling point and is seen here with the centre hose trailing as two Royal Navy aircraft – Sea Vixen FAW.2 XN685 and Buccaneer S.1 XN976 – refuel from the Mk 20B wing pods during a flight in late 1965. (*Crown Copyright/Air Historical Branch image T-5927*)

No. 90 Squadron Valiant BK.1, XD813, based at RAF Honington, photographed while refuelling Vulcan
1A XH498, from RAF Waddington, in May 1962. (*Crown Copyright/Air Historical Branch image T-3164a*)

V-Bomber Conversions: Valiant, Vulcan and Victor

ollowing the end of the Second World War, the British Government formulated the British
omic weapons programme and the associated nuclear deterrent policies. The atomic bomb
rogramme formally began with Air Staff Operational Requirement OR.1001, which was issued
August 1946 and envisaged a weapon not to exceed 24 ft 2 in. in length, 5 ft in diameter,
),000 lb in weight, and suitable for release from 20,000 to 50,000 ft.

Around the same time, the Air Ministry drew up requirements for bombers to replace the
cisting piston-powered heavy bombers then in service with Bomber Command, including
e Avro Lancaster and Avro Lincoln. The Air Ministry distributed Specification B.35/46 to
number of aviation companies to satisfy Air Staff Operational Requirement OR.229 for a
Medium-range bomber landplane capable of carrying one 10,000 lb bomb to a target 1,500 nm
om a base which may be anywhere in the world'. Further requirements included a cruising
Deed of 500 knots at heights between 35,000 and 50,000 feet. The weapon load was to include
single 10,000 lb 'Special gravity bomb' (i.e. a free-fall nuclear weapon) or, over shorter ranges,
),000 lb of conventional bombs. No defensive weapons were to be carried as the aircraft had
rely on its speed and altitude!

A similar Air Staff Operational Requirement OR.230 was also issued which required a
ong-range bomber' with a 2,000 n.m. radius of action operating at a height of 50,000 feet,
cruising speed of 575 mph and a maximum weight of 200,000 lb. Responses to this latter
quirement were submitted by Short Brothers, Bristol and Handley Page. However, the Air
inistry recognised that development costs to meet such stringent requirements would be very

significant for an aircraft that would ultimately be required in very small – and uneconomic quantities; and that most 'targets' would not require such a long range. They also issued a les demanding requirement for a 'Medium-range bomber' to Air Ministry Specification B.35/4 Requiring the same 10,000 lb payload and 575 mph cruising speed, at heights of 45,000 t 50,000 ft, but now with a target range of just 1,500 n.m.

The Handley Page HP.80 (later Victor) and Avro Type 698 (later Vulcan) were considere the best two of the proposed designs to Specification B.35/46 and orders were placed for tw prototypes of each. However, it was also recognised that both designs were – even for th time – cutting edge and somewhat high-risk, so an order was also placed for the Vickers desig (later Valiant). Although it did not meet the requirements in full, the design posed few risks (failure and could enter service earlier than the other two chosen designs.

Valiant

With the prototype (WB210) making its first flight on 18 May 1951, the Valiant B.1 was become the first of the four-jet V-Bombers to enter service with the RAF. Eventually, fou types of the Valiant would enter service: the B.1 bomber; the B(PR).1 bomber or photograph reconnaissance; the B(K).1 flight-refuelling receiver aircraft (bomber or tanker role); and th B(PR)K.1 flight-refuelling receiver for bomber, photographic reconnaissance or tanker roles.

The first squadron to receive the Valiant aircraft was No. 138 Squadron at RAF Gaydon i January 1955. Later, the Valiant was operated by No. 232 OCU and Nos 7, 18, 49, 90, 138, 148, 19 207, 214 and 543 Squadrons.

However, a paper researched and written by C. H. Latimer-Needham, the Chief Engineer (Flight Refuelling Ltd, would have a profound effect on the nuclear deterrent fleet of Valia aircraft and the way they needed to operate. He identified that the B9/48 aircraft with i operational radius would only be able to strike against a limited number of the necessary Sovi targets, effectively undermining the overall impact of the deterrent. What the force required become completely effective was a force of tanking support aircraft. All of the existing aircra available for tanking were considered to be too slow for the task so the ideal airframe for the jc was... another Valiant! Eventually, the military powers sat up and took notice. While the Valia had never been intended to have an in-flight refuelling capability, this eventually became th most important retrospective modification the type was to receive.

Two aircraft (WZ376 as tanker and WZ390 as receiver) were set aside from the programm and delivered to Flight Refuelling Ltd to conduct AAR trials. Initial teething troubles we encountered, particularly with the HDU and hard drogue, but all were eventually overcome.

The first unit to receive Valiant aircraft fitted out for flight refuelling was No. 214 Squadro at Marham in early 1959, and who proceeded to undertake a number of long-distance trainin flights to prove the system's effectiveness. At the time, only other Valiant aircraft were able receive fuel, but by October 1959 a No. 101 Squadron Vulcan took on fuel. By the end of 195 No. 214 Squadron was considered fully operational as a flight-refuelling squadron.

The second squadron equipped with Valiant tankers was No. 90 at RAF Honington. By no other receivers of fuel had included a variety of Lightning fighters as well as USAF RB-6(Destroyer aircraft. As a tanker, the Valiant acquitted itself well and much of Nos 214 an 90 Squadrons' work was bread-and-butter tanking; but they also undertook a great deal of tria work with a variety of receiver aircraft.

The Valiant was a faithful servant but in mid-1964, some aircraft were found to have fatign cracks in the front and rear wing spars. On 6 August 1965, Valiant B.1 WP217 from No. 232 OC uffered a rear spar failure during a high-speed flight over North Wales. The aircraft was arefully flown back to Gaydon and completed a successful flapless approach and landing. The ircraft was in a very poor condition and a closer inspection revealed a multitude of fatigue roblems despite the fact that the aircraft had only flown 2,330 hours, just 55 per cent of its esigned fatigue life.

The entire fleet was inspected and afterwards only twelve were deemed 'fit to fly', although ineteen were available to fly 'in a national emergency'. A repair scheme was planned but when ie first aircraft was dismantled at No. 19 MU, St Athan, the fatigue problems were more severe ian first thought. A proposal to re-spar the entire fleet was flatly refused on the grounds of cost nd so, from 26 January 1965 onwards, the Valiant aircraft were basically scrapped where they ad landed.

From the RAF's perspective, the loss of the Valiant was not desperate because the type had ome to be seen as 'elderly' and both Victor and Vulcan aircraft were available to fill the gaps – in ie bombing, strategic reconnaissance and, eventually, the AAR roles.

ictor

Orders for the Handley Page HP.80 (later Victor) were placed at the same time as the Valiant, ith the first prototype (WB771) flying on 24 December 1952. The first production Victor B.1 XA917) made its maiden flight on 1 February 1956, with the first B.1 entering squadron service ith No. 232 OCU at Gaydon on 28 November 1957. The first operational unit, No. 10 Squadron, t Cottesmore, received its first Victor aircraft in April 1958. Deliveries of the improved B.1A ontinued with the aircraft eventually being in service with four squadrons, within two Wings f the force.

The Victor B.2 marked a significant advance on the earlier variant with a greater wing pan and the improved Rolls-Royce Conway engines. A noticeable external change was the nstallation of large trailing edge fairings on the wing as an aid to low-level performance. The .2 first entered service with No. 232 OCU at Gaydon in October 1961 and was followed into perational service with No. 139 Squadron at Wittering in February 1962. Orders were placed for ifty-one B.2 aircraft, reduced to thirty-four in August 1960. The last B.2 (XM718) was delivered ） the RAF on 2 May 1963.

From December 1965, the Victor SR.2 entered service with No. 542 Squadron at Wyton and ecame Bomber Command's standard strategic reconnaissance aircraft, replacing the Valiant ·(PR).1 in service.

By the end of 1968, the Victor B.2R aircraft was starting to be withdrawn from service, lthough the SR.2 variants continued until May 1974. However, it did not signal the end for the eautiful Victor aircraft, merely a new beginning.

ictor Tankers

With the sudden loss of the Valiant tanker fleet in 1965, the RAF was forced to accelerate plans or the introduction of the Victor as a tanker. Victor B.1 aircraft had been collected at Radlett rom the disbanded Cottesmore Wing ready for conversion, while awaiting a final decision on ie tanker Production Specification. However, the urgent need for tankers required an interim neasure to be operational as soon as possible.

Two tanker versions had already been evaluated at Boscombe Down using XA918 and oth featured additional fuel tanks inside the bomb bay. One incorporated a pair of nder-wing-mounted FRL Mk 20A HDUs, each one mounted on a pylon attached to the under-wing fuel tank strong point, which would have provided a two-point tanker with the leas amount of modification work. However, trials conducted at Boscombe Down showed that wit this arrangement, the pods were far too inboard, taking the receiver aircraft dangerously close t the tanker's tail, while also failing to provide sufficient safety margin between the two receiver Consequently, the decision was taken to move the pods farther outboard but to accept this optio would delay the conversion process. The other layout was for a single FRL Mk 17 HDU mounte at the rear of the Victor's bomb bay.

A third option, and the one eventually chosen, was to combine the two schemes to produce three-point tanker, with the fuselage HDU available to larger aircraft and the under-wing pods b the smaller fast jets. XA918 appeared in this configuration during the 1964 Farnborough Air Sho\

While plans were being considered for the three-point tanker, work began on the conversio of a number of Victor B.1A aircraft into B(K).1A two-point tankers, which were urgently require in the support of the UK's Air Defence – particularly with regard to the Lightning F.3 aircra actively engaged on QRA duties, which struggled to remain on station for any length of tim without the support of a tanker aircraft. These conversions had a pair of under-wing-mounte FRL Mk 20B HDUs and bomb-bay fuel tanks but retained their bombing capabilities, if require

The first conversion was XH620, which made its first flight on 28 April 1965 and was soo followed by the remaining five conversions, all destined for No. 55 Squadron.

While this work had been underway, plans to convert Victor B.1 and B.1A aircraft int three-point tankers (the K.1 and K.1A respectively) were gaining ground. Eventually, ten of th planned fourteen aircraft were duly converted. This work was far more complex as, in additio to the under-wing Mk 20B HDUs, it also involved removing the bomb-bay and offensive ear warning equipment to make room for the FRL Mk 17 HDU that was mounted just behind th bomb-bay. The first three-point tanker conversion was K.1A XA937, which flew on 2 Novembe 1965 and was soon delivered to the A&AEE at Boscombe Down for service trials. Aircra continued to flow from the conversion line and were initially delivered to No. 57 Squadron, wit others joining No. 214 Squadron.

When No. 55 Squadron eventually received its three-point tankers, it passed its remainin two-point tanker to the Tanker Training Flight (TTF) that had been formed at Marham i January 1967.

Victor B.2

The next proposal for the Victor tanker was the three-point K.2, featuring the more powerfu Rolls-Royce Conway 201 engines which in turn provided a greater fuel load and improved take-o performance, especially when operating from 'hot-and-high' airfields. The K.2 would also featur fixed under-wing slipper tanks. Weight was going to be a potential problem with the K.2 so plan were made to remove any unnecessary equipment, including the early warning equipment an chaff dispenser, along with any associated wiring not required for the tanking role.

Unfortunately, no Victor B.2 aircraft were available for conversion until the disbandment c the Wittering squadrons, scheduled for the end of 1968. However, Victor SR.2 XM715 had bee under repair at Radlett following wing damage so the programme was able to commence wit this aircraft as a trials installation for the K.2 programme.

A shortage of finance eventually reduced the programme to twenty-four aircraft, but befor the programme could get under way Handley Page ran into financial difficulties and went int liquidation on 27 February 1970. The actual conversion contract for the K.2 programme was awarde to Hawker Siddeley, and the aircraft were flown from Radlett to Woodford between July and Augus

The first Victor K.2 converted at Woodford was XL231, which made its maiden flight on March 1972. It was not modified to full production standard and after initial flight testing it was delivered to the A&AEE at Boscombe Down for service trials. Once completed, XL231 was returned to Woodford for full conversion and eventually delivered to Marham. The first aircraft to be delivered to the RAF was XL233, which joined No. 232 OCU in May 1974.

The first squadron to receive the Victor K.2 was No. 55 Squadron, which formally converted on 1 July 1975 and was followed by No. 57 Squadron during the summer of 1976. Because of the relatively small number of Victor B.2 conversions, No. 214 Squadron retained its K.1 and K.1A aircraft until Nos 55 and 57 became fully operational, then disbanded on 28 January 1977.

Popular Warrior

Despite having operated through some of the most difficult Cold War periods, the Victor bomber was never called into action. Ironically, the first time it did see action was during Operation Corporate, as a tanker aircraft. However, its significant contribution to the Falklands War cannot be underestimated. It also made a major contribution to the first Gulf War when Victor K.2 aircraft of No. 55 Squadron were deployed to Muharraq, Bahrain, in support of both RAF and coalition forces. Further details of these activities, along with the later Operation Warden, can be found in Chapter 6, pages 82–96.

During its peacetime tanking duties, the Victor K.2 became the backbone of the RAF's tanker fleet and was a popular supplier of fuel, especially with the fast jet receivers, including the Lightning. Its ability to fly high and fast while dispensing fuel was always welcomed.

Sadly, it was its role in the various conflicts that would have a decimating effect on its remaining airframe fatigue life. After completing a deployment to Akrotiri in support of RAF Jaguars operating reconnaissance missions over northern Iraq and another deployment to Muharraq in support of aircraft monitoring the Gulf ceasefire agreement which lasted until September 1993, all of the Victor airframes were returned to Marham in readiness for the type's withdrawal from service, planned for the following year. No. 55 Squadron was eventually disbanded on 15 October 1993 and ended the Victor's long and illustrious career with the RAF. Thankfully, most Victor K.2 aircraft were disposed of to preservation groups and two aircraft remain in a 'running' condition, at Bruntingthorpe and Elvington.

Vulcan

The Vulcan B.1 entered service with Bomber Command in 1956, initially equipping No. 230 OCU at Waddington. The first operational squadron was No. 83, also at Waddington, in 1957. With the Vulcan B.1 in full production, the design team began to make significant improvements, in particular with a larger wing and more powerful 17,000 lb static thrust Olympus 200 engines in prospect. The first production Vulcan B.2 made its initial flight on 19 August 1958. The B.2 entered service on 1 July 1960, once again with No. 230 OCU and in October with No. 83 Squadron. Vulcan B.2 production totalled eighty-nine aircraft and ended with XM657 in December 1964.

The only time the Vulcan saw action was during the memorable Black Buck operations, the ultra long-range strike against the Argentinean force occupying the Falklands, refuelled by Victor tankers (see Chapter 6, pages 84–5).

As the Falklands War was coming to an end, the B.2 was reaching the end of its service life. However, the Falklands War had consumed significant quantities of fatigue hours from the Victor K.2 airframes. Orders had been placed in 1979 for VC10 K.2 and K.3 tanker aircraft, with Tristar tanker/transport aircraft ordered in February 1983, but a stop-gap was immediately required before the new types came into service.

With the tanking support for the UK Air Defence and its NATO commitments being stretched to, and probably beyond, its limits (although with USAF KC-135A support, it was maintained) a decision was taken on 4 May 1982 to convert six of the remaining Vulcan B.2 aircraft into single-point tankers, with British Aerospace at Woodford being the major contractor. Interestingly, a decision to convert six Hercules C.1 aircraft into C.1K tankers at Marshall of Cambridge was taken around the same time, although the latter decision was made in connection with the ongoing support of the Falkland Islands.

A single second-hand Mk 17B HDU was installed into the rear fuselage and an additional bomb-bay fuel tank added to the two already in existence, providing the Vulcan with almost 100,000 lb (45,000 kg) of fuel.

Just fifty days after being ordered, the first Vulcan K.2, XH561, was delivered to No. 50 Squadron at RAF Waddington. In the coming months, the remaining five aircraft were also delivered to this squadron, where they operated until finally being withdrawn from service in March 1984, although interestingly, they were never deployed overseas.

The six aircraft converted were: XH558, XH560, XH561, XJ825, XL445 and XM571.

WZ376 was the first Valiant B(PR)K.1 converted by Vickers to tanker 'Type 758' and, following manufacturer's trials, had under-wing fuel tanks fitted in February 1957. It was photographed during refuelling trials in 1957 with the hose and drogue extended from its bomb bay-mounted FRL Mk 16 refuelling pod. (*Vickers Aircraft image MP670? via Brooklands Museum*)

On 9 July 1959, a Valiant of No. 214 Squadron carried out the first non-stop flight from the UK to Cape Town (6,060 miles in 11 hours and 28 minutes) with the aid of air-to-air refuelling. This image was released in August 1959 and shows two aircraft of RAF Marham-based No. 214 Squadron – Valiant B(K).1 XD870 refuelling Valiant B.1 WZ390. (*Crown Copyright/ Air Historical Branch image PRB-1-16962*)

Valiant BK.1 XD816 of No. 214 Squadron trails its centreline hose while awaiting a pair of No. 23 Squadron Javelin FAW.9s (XH886/C and XH887/F) in October 1960. It is likely that this image was taken during early tanking trials and training for the Javelin fleet. (*Crown Copyright/Air Historical Branch image PRB-1-19711*)

In late 1960, Vulcan crews started to undertake a series of refuelling trials ahead of a proposed non-stop flight from the UK to Australia. This photograph, taken on 15 December 1960, shows Valiant BK.1 XD859 of No. 214 Squadron refuelling No. 617 Squadron Vulcan B.1A XH506. The FRL Mk 16 refuelling package can be clearly seen, located in the bomb bay of the tanker. (*Crown Copyright/Air Historical Branch image PRB-1-20296*)

A Valiant BK.1, XD812, of No. 214 Squadron refuels a Lightning F.1A, XM173/P, from No. 56 Squadron based at RAF Wattisham. (*Crown Copyright/Air Historical Branch image PRB-1-23521*)

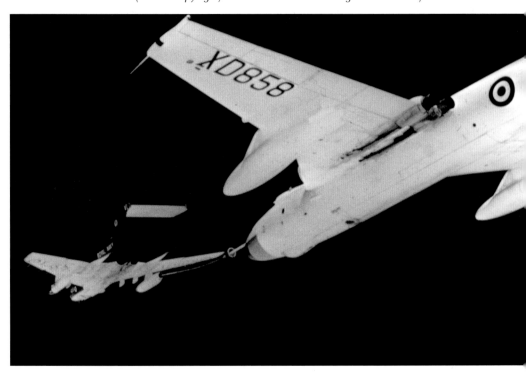

The rather unusual sight of a Fleet Air Arm Sea Vixen FAW.1 refuelling a Valiant BK.1, XD858, using the FRL Mk 20 refuelling pod mounted on the underside of the starboard wing, while an additional fuel tank was installed under the port wing of the tanker. This image may well have been taken in 1962 when No. 899 NAS were trialling the Mk 20 buddy-buddy pod installation on the Sea Vixen FAW.1. (*Brooklands Museum image SeaVixenRefuellingValiant*)

A close-up view of Wattisham-based No. 56 Squadron Lightning F.1A XM179 as it refuels from a Valiant BK.1, XD816, of No. 214 Squadron in 1963. Sadly, XM179 was later lost in a collision with another No. 56 Squadron Lightning at Great Bricett, Suffolk, on 6 June 1963. (*Crown Copyright/Air Historical Branch image T-4280*)

Having been originally constructed as a Victor B.1 at Radlett by Handley Page in 1956, it later became the very first prototype two-point tanker conversion with the addition of a pair of under-wing-mounted FRL Mk 20B HDUs, and made its first flight as a K.1 in 1964. It was soon undergoing AAR trials with the A&AEE at Boscombe Down and was photographed refuelling a pair of Lightning F.2 aircraft (XN784/L and XN730/B) of No. 19 Squadron, RAF Leconfield, in 1965. (*Crown Copyright/Air Historical Branch image T-5421*)

Treasury approval for the Victor K.1A three-point tanker was finally given in November 1963 and initially six two-point tankers were hastily converted in an attempt to make up part of the tanker shortfall following the loss of the Valiant fleet. Work was conducted by Handley Page at Radlett, with the first – XA937, a former B.1 airframe – making its first post-conversion flight as a K.1 on 2 November 1965. Later, all conversions, including XH618 shown here, were converted from B.1A airframes into K.1A three-point tankers. XH618 was photographed in June 1970 in its No. 57 Squadron markings. (*Crown Copyright/Air Historical Branch image TN-1-6232-39*)

Only ten Short Belfast C.1 long-range strategic freighter aircraft were ordered, with XR371 *Enceladus* being the final aircraft to fly. The aircraft was photographed while undergoing AAR fuelling trials with the A&AEE at Boscombe Down, refuelling on this occasion from an unidentified No.57 Squadron Victor K.1A. (*Crown Copyright/Air Historical Branch image AAEE-944-1*)

Victor K.2 XL233 was the first K.2 conversion to be returned to RAF service when it was delivered to No. 232 OCU at RAF Marham. It was photographed shortly afterwards demonstrating its three-point tanker capability with all three AAR hoses trailed. (*Crown Copyright/Air Historical Branch image TN-1-7013-15*)

In May 1971 a party of Canadian Armed Forces (CAF) personnel were hosted at RAF Marham by No. 55 Squadron to conduct AAR refuelling trials with RAF Victor K.2 aircraft and its hose and drogue refuelling system. A CAF CF-116, serial number 116750, was photographed refuelling from Victor K.2 XH588 on 12 May 1971. CF-116 116755 was awaiting its turn in the background. (*Crown Copyright/Air Historical Branch image TN-1-6385-28*)

Four Phantom FGR.2 aircraft of No. 29 Squadron, RAF Coningsby, refuel from Victor K.1 XA936 of No. 214 Squadron in January 1975. (*Crown Copyright/Air Historical Branch imageTN-1-7136-18*)

Panavia MRCA (later Tornado) 'P02' XX946 photographed during an AAR trial from Victor K.2 XL191 in 1975. (*BAE Systems Heritage Collection image AWCN3523*)

Nimrod MR.2P XV238 photographed while refuelling from an unidentified Victor K.2 of No. 57 Squadron on 21 August 1982. (*BAE Systems Heritage Collection image 14-1-821*)

Farewell to the Victor tanker. This image was taken just days before No. 55 Squadron was stood down at RAF Marham and all of the remaining Victor K.2 aircraft were withdrawn, with most being preserved in museums across the UK. This image shows XL190 crossing the north Norfolk coast en route to Marham after completion of a practice passing-out parade fly-by. XL190 was delivered to RAF St Mawgan, where it languished until being scrapped in 1999. The cockpit section was last noted at Manston. (*Keith Wilson*)

XM571, one of just six Vulcan B.2 bombers converted for the air-to-air refuelling role, pictured trailing its single refuelling hose during operational trials. Although the aircraft wears the badge of No. 101 Squadron on the tail, all tanker Vulcan aircraft served with No. 50 Squadron at RAF Waddington. (*Crown Copyright/Air Historical Branch image TN-1-9370-8*)

A Vulcan B.2 refuelling a pair of No. 228 OCU Phantom FGR.2 receivers during a late-afternoon tow line off the north-east coast of the UK. (*Crown Copyright/Air Historical Branch image AHB-Slide-CGY-PHA-13*)

No. 50 Squadron Vulcan
2 at RAF Waddington in
ugust 1983. The refurbished
17B HDUs fitted to the
ar fuselage of the Vulcan
2 can be seen during
utine maintenance to the
craft. (*Crown Copyright/
Historical Branch image
1-9508-8*)

Vulcan K.2 aircraft buddy-buddy tanking! A pair of No. 50 Squadron Vulcan K.2 aircraft during an AAR
training sortie. XH561 is the tanker, while XH560 is the receiver. (*BAE Systems Heritage image K-2-465*)

Second-Hand Airliners and the Hastily Converted Hercules

On 2 April 1982, the military forces of Argentina invaded the Falkland Islands. During the afternoon 30 April, representatives of Marshall's of Cambridge met with the MoD to discuss the urgent conversi of an initial batch of four Hercules C.1 aircraft into single-point tankers utilising a FRL Mk 17B refuelli package. The first aircraft – XV296 – was delivered to Cambridge on 1 May for work to commence a made its first post-conversion test flight on 8 June and re-entered squadron service at Lyneham on 5 J 1982, just seventy-six days after the go-ahead was given. A further two tanker aircraft conversions we later ordered and one of that six-aircraft package was XV201, which was photographed in June 19 while demonstrating its single-point tanker capability. (*Crown Copyright/Air Historical Branch ima DPR-792-128*)

Vickers VC10 K.2 and K.3 Aircraft

An AAR tanker variant of the VC10 had long been sought by Air Staff as far back as t mid-1960s. The British Aircraft Corporation (BAC) had undertaken a variety of design studi which confirmed the viability of the requirement, including the conversion of former airlin aircraft, if they became available.

In 1977, a number of airframes did become available. Firstly, following the financial failu of the East African Airways Corporation (EAA), four of the original five Super VC10 aircraft storage at Nairobi were repossessed on behalf of the lessor by BAC. They were flown back to t UK and placed into storage at Filton. In October and November 1977, five former British Airwa (BA) and Gulf Air VC10s were withdrawn from service and became available to the project.

In March 1978, a contract was awarded to the BAe Aircraft Group at Filton to undertake t work, with the detailed design leadership at Weybridge – where most of the original VC10 desi staff were still present.

The main features of the K.2 (Standard VC10) and K.3 (Super VC10) conversion programme were:

- A centreline FRL Mk 17B hose drum unit (HDU) with a high fuel transfer rate (500 gallons (2,250 litres) per minute) for the refuelling of large aircraft was installed.
- Two wing-mounted FRL Mk 32 AAR pods, each capable of delivering 275 gallons (1,238 litres) of fuel per minute, were added.
- Five additional fuel tanks were installed into the former cabin, mounted on a strengthened floor (a relatively easy task on the K.3 aircraft as they featured the large forward-fuselage freight door, but a significantly more complex task on the K.2 aircraft, which required sections of the fuselage to be removed in order to gain access).
- A permanently mounted 9-foot-long nose-mounted AAR in-flight refuelling probe was installed.
- A common engine – the Rolls-Royce RCo.43 Mk 301 Conway – was installed into both variants.
- A Turboméca Artouste APU was mounted in the fuselage tailcone (as previously fitted to the RAF VC10 C.1 variants).
- CCTV was installed under the centre fuselage in a cupola capable of observing both centreline HDU and wing pods.
- A suite of military avionics was added.
- A Flight Engineer-operated AAR HDU and wing pod control panel and CCTV monitor were installed.

The first conversion, K.2 ZA141, made its first flight at Filton on 22 June 1982 in a rather strange green/grey camouflage, earning itself the nickname 'The Lizard'.

Development work continued at Boscombe Down and, once cleared to enter squadron service, was repainted into the then-standard all-over hemp colour scheme. The first VC10 K.2 delivered into service was ZA140, which was flown to Brize Norton on 25 July 1983 to join the new Tanker Training Flight (TTF), officially formed on 1 August 1983 as part of No. 241 OCU.

No. 101 Squadron was then formed at Brize Norton, on 1 May 1984, while deliveries of the converted aircraft continued and tasking commenced. The first K.3 – ZA150 – was delivered on February 1985, with the last conversion – K.3 ZA148 – being delivered on 27 March 1986 and, doing so, brought No. 101 Squadron up to a full operating strength of nine airframes.

First Class Reputation

The newly formed No. 101 Squadron quickly earned a wonderful reputation for themselves and were regarded by many military operators as one of the very best air-to-air refuelling squadrons across the globe – a reputation aided by the reliability of the VC10. Much of this was gained from its military exploits (see Chapter 6, pages 82–96) although its peacetime operations are still highly regarded, especially by the fast jet pilots it refuelled on a daily basis. Most of their bread-and-butter operations were conducted in special Air-to-Air Refuelling Areas (AARAs) around the UK, strategically located over the sea. Within the AARAs, the VC10s would operate 'tow-lines', normally flown in a race track pattern, while providing fuel to the RAF's fast-jet assets, prolonging their sortie length and therefore maximising their training opportunities and defensive effectiveness.

Hercules C.1K

With the existing fleet of Victor K.2 tanker aircraft being so heavily committed during the Falklands conflict, an urgent requirement arose for an additional tanker aircraft. Following

discussions between Marshall's of Cambridge and the MoD, it was decided to convert s⬛
Hercules C.1 aircraft into C.1K single-point tankers, as well as a similar number of surpl⬛
Vulcan B.2 aircraft. The former would provide additional support to the Falkland Islands wh⬛
the latter would provide all-important cover and support in the air defence role around the U⬛

Both aircraft would require the installation of a single FRL Mk 17B refuelling package and⬛
search was instigated for any surviving units!

Once all of the requirements had been agreed by 5 May 1982, initial orders for the componen⬛
were placed. On 1 May, XV296 had been delivered to Cambridge for the first conversion. C⬛
3 May, and following a series of meetings between Marshall's and FRL, the decision was tak⬛
to mount the Mk 17B unit onto a framework that could then be fitted onto the lower cargo ram⬛
In addition, four former Andover auxiliary fuel tanks were installed into each tanker, providi⬛
an additional 2,800 lb (350 Imp Gallons, 15,750 litres) in each tank for a total of 11,200 addition⬛
pounds of fuel available for transfer. However, these tanks could not be filled from the aircraf⬛
existing ground refuelling points but instead required a fuel bowser, with the trigger nozzle ⬛
the refuelling hose having to refill each tank individually.

The first tanker conversion was completed on 25 May and prepared for ground and flig⬛
testing, which commenced at the A&AEE Boscombe Down on 4 June. Following initial problem⬛
in these early trials, the aircraft was returned to Marshall's for modifications. Initial wet contac⬛
were made with the A&AEE's Buccaneer aircraft on 21 June and the acceptance trials continu⬛
on the following day. The first aircraft was delivered to RAF Lyneham on 5 July, just seventy-s⬛
calendar days after the go-ahead had been given. Three further tankers were delivered ⬛
19, 21 and 26 July. The final pair were also flown into Lyneham and entered service short⬛
afterwards. It was an astonishing achievement by all involved in the programme, but especia⬛
the Marshall's of Cambridge team!

The six aircraft that underwent conversion into single-point tankers were: XV201, XV2(⬛
XV204, XV213, XV192 and XV296.

On 15 October 1982, the first two aircraft were placed into service and spent time operati⬛
around the Falkland Islands, where aircraft serving on detachment to No. 1312 (In-Fligl⬛
Refuelling) Flight provided tanker support to Harrier GR.3, Phantom FGR.2 and Tornado I⬛
aircraft of No. 1435 Flight in the air defence of the islands. They remained in service with t⬛
Flight until withdrawn from service in the Falklands on 31 March 1996. XV204 left the Falklan⬛
on 26 March 1996, with XV214 being the last to leave on the following day.

Once all six Hercules C.1K aircraft had been withdrawn from service, they were initia⬛
placed into storage at Cambridge. XV203 and XV213 were later sold to the Sri Lankan A⬛
Force as CR-880 and CR-881 respectively. A third airframe, XV201, was allotted the ser⬛
CR-882 but was never delivered. Instead it was broken up at Cambridge, with the fusela⬛
section being moved to Porton Down as a ground instructional airframe. The remaining thr⬛
airframes were also scrapped, with the last to succumb to the axe being XV296, which w⬛
scrapped by July 2003.

VC10 K.4

In addition to the purchase of the former BA and Gulf Air 'standard' VC10 fleet, the R⬛
purchased the entire fleet of the fourteen remaining Super VC10 aircraft from British Airwa⬛
on their retirement from airline service in 1981. During April and May, eleven were ferried⬛
RAF Abingdon for long-term storage while the remaining three were flown to Brize Norton f⬛
spares recovery and as ground instructional airframes.

Funding for the conversion programme was a difficult and protracted affair, and the aircraft suffered badly from the elements as a result of the significant delays.

In 1989, the long-awaited approval for additional VC10 tanking capability (in the form of the K.4 and C.1K variants) was finally forthcoming in the form of Staff Requirement (Air) 415 ASR415), which covered the conversion of the five remaining former British Airways Super VC10s, then held in storage at Abingdon, into three-point tankers with the designation K.4.

After having been put out to tender, the work was finally won by BAe at Manchester, with a contract issued in January 1990. The aircraft were prepared for a single flight to Filton for the conversion programme to commence. The first VC10 to undergo the K.4 programme was ZD242. The programme was very similar to the earlier K.3 programme although the addition of the five fuselage-mounted fuel tanks was excluded on economic grounds. Instead, the passenger compartment was retained although the seating was reversed to the usual RAF standard.

The first flight was made by ZD242 on 29 July 1993 and, following test flying by BAe, was transferred to the A&AEE at Boscombe Down. The first K.4 was delivered to No. 101 Squadron on 28 April 1994 with the final conversion – ZD235 – arriving at Brize Norton on 8 March 1996.

VC10 C.1K

Simultaneously with the K.4 programme, ASR415 also covered approval for eight VC10 C.1 passenger/transport aircraft then operated by No. 10 Squadron at Brize Norton to undergo conversion to two-point tankers with the addition of a pair of under-wing-mounted FRL Mk 32 HDUs. After the bidding process was completed, an agreement was reached for the conversion work to be undertaken by Flight Refuelling Limited at Bournemouth/Hurn Airport, on a subcontract basis to BAe. This contract was later increased to cover all thirteen of the remaining C.1 fleet.

The first C.1K conversion began on 28 February 1991 when XV101 was flown into Hurn from Brize Norton. The first C.1K delivered back to No. 10 Squadron was XV103. The last C.1K conversion – XV808 – was delivered to No. 10 Squadron on 7 February 1997.

This now provided a tanker force consisting of twenty-seven VC10 airframes, although this strength did not remain long as some of the earlier K.2 conversions were already reaching the end of their design life.

Tristar Conversions

Following one of the lessons learned from the Falklands War, of the absolute indispensability of a suitable strategic air-to-air refuelling fleet, the RAF sought to find a suitable airframe to provide the capability. In addition, they also required a new strategic long-range transport aircraft to maintain communications with the RAF's new base on the Falkland Islands. Both problems could be resolved by acquiring the former British Airways fleet of six Lockheed L.1101 Tristar 500 airliners and having them converted into strategic tanker/transport aircraft.

At the time, the Victor K.2 tankers were rapidly approaching the end of their fatigue lives and the stopgap fleet of six hastily converted Vulcan K.2 aircraft had very limited fatigue lives themselves. The 'new' VC10 K.2 and K.3 aircraft were beginning to enter service with No. 101 Squadron at Brize Norton but these aircraft were more suited to the tactical tanking role, particularly in support of the UK air defence capability.

The decision to purchase the six former British Airways Tristar 500 aircraft was announced on 14 December 1982 and the contract for the conversion awarded to Marshall's of Cambridge in February 1983. Initially, a contract was awarded for six aircraft to be converted, although this was later increased to nine aircraft with the acquisition of three former Pan American Air Lines Tristar aircraft in 1984, which were converted to C.2 and C.2A passenger aircraft.

The conversion to tanker/transport aircraft was a massive undertaking for Marshall's, especially with the fitting of two large auxiliary fuel tanks in the underfloor cargo compartments, providing around 100,000 lb of additional fuel. The refuelling equipment chosen was a pair of FRL Mk 17T hose drum units mounted in tandem within a new pressurised cell at the base of the rear fuselage. The aircraft was required to have a single-point tanker capability but the fitting of two HDUs provided a comforting redundancy, especially on long-distance strategic tanking missions.

Two airframes (ZD952 and ZD948) were initially converted to C.1 status and delivered to RAF Brize Norton on 4 July 1983 and 13 July 1983 respectively. Both were later returned to Cambridge for conversion to K.1 tanker status.

The first aircraft to undergo full conversion to KC.1 status was ZD950, which was then delivered to the A&AEE at Boscombe Down to conduct acceptance trials. However, the first fully converted aircraft delivered to No. 216 Squadron was KC.1 ZD953, which was formally handed over to the RAF on 24 March 1986, during a ceremony at Cambridge. It was delivered to No. 216 Squadron at Brize Norton two days later.

Interestingly, at the acceptance ceremony at Cambridge, Sir Joseph Gilbert, the Deputy C-in-C Strike Command, said:

> ...with the support of a VC10 tanker, we can keep three Phantoms on station prepared to intercept Soviet aircraft 650nm north of Scotland for two hours but now, with a Tristar we can keep 12 Phantoms similarly deployed. When deploying aircraft to the Middle East and beyond, via Akrotiri in Cyprus, a Victor tanker could take two Phantoms to Akrotiri but the tanker itself would have to land in Italy, whereas a Tristar could now take four Phantoms to Cyprus, plus 150 passengers and 5,000lb in freight with the Tristar itself landing at Akrotiri.

All of the Tristar fleet were delivered to and operated by No. 216 Squadron at RAF Brize Norton. In addition to demonstrating its capabilities on strategic tanker/transport operations in peacetime, the aircraft served in a number of theatres including the first Gulf War, Kosovo and Afghanistan. More information on these activities can be found in Chapter 6, pages 82–96.

The Tristar was expected to remain in RAF service until 2010, but this was extended through to 2014 under the Strategic Defence and Security Review conducted in 2010. On 20 March 2014 No. 216 Squadron was disbanded and all nine aircraft flown into Bruntingthorpe, where they are currently held in storage while receiving regular maintenance. It is hoped that at least five of the aircraft will be flown to the USA and enter service with a civilian contractor in support of US military tanking activities. The remaining aircraft are likely to be reduced to spares in support of them.

Tristar Conversions and Types

RAF Serial	Mark	Role	Previous Identity	Previous Operator
ZD948	K.1	Tanker/Passenger	G-BFCA	British Airways
ZD949	K.1	Tanker/Passenger	G-BFCB	British Airways
ZD950	KC.1	Tanker/Freight	G-BFCC	British Airways
ZD951	K.1	Tanker/Passenger	G-BFCD	British Airways
ZD952	KC.1	Tanker/Freight	G-BFCE	British Airways
ZD953	KC.1	Tanker/Freight	G-BFCF	British Airways

ZE704	C.2	Passenger	N508	Pan American AL
ZE705	C.2	Passenger	N509	Pan American AL
ZE706	C.2A	Passenger	N503	Pan American AL

Farewell to the VC10

On 8 July 1998, the Strategic Defence Review announced the end of both the VC10 and Tristar operations. They were to be replaced by a new, yet-to-be-identified type, chosen after a thorough review. That review would subsequently identify the Air Tanker Consortium bid as the Future Strategic Tanker Aircraft (FSTA), with the Airbus A330 MRTT Voyager.

Following the arrival of the C.1K and K.4 variants into the tanker fleet, it was time to say farewell to the five K.2 airframes. ZA143 was the first to leave and was flown to St Athan on 21 August 1998 for a 'spares recovery programme'. ZA142 was the last to leave Brize Norton and arrived at St Athan on 27 March 2001. Some of the older C.1Ks were also involved in this programme, with XV103 arriving at St Athan on 11 December 2001.

The final fleet drawdown commenced on 6 April 2010 when the first two (XR807 and XV109) of the remaining fifteen aircraft were flown to Bruntingthorpe. The very last VC10 flight was made on 25 October 2013, when ZA147 was retired into Bruntingthorpe, ending forty-one years of VC10 operations with the RAF.

The trial installation of the FRL Mk 17T HDU onto the side of the Hercules cargo ramp was photographed while the conversion work was being undertaken at Cambridge Airport. (*Marshall's of Cambridge*)

The tanker conversion also included the installation of four auxiliary fuel tanks that had previously been installed in the Andover; each tank had a capacity to provide a further 2,800 lbs of fuel. (*Marshall's of Cambridge*)

Three Hercules C.1K tanker conversions were photographed on the ramp at Cambridge in July 1982, including XV201 and XV298. The positions of the drogue and the refuelling traffic lights fitted to XV201 are clear in this image. (*Marshall's of Cambridge image MCE-54-9385*)

Hercules C.1K XV296 refuels a standard Hercules C.1P (XV200) on 24 June 1982, during accelerated flight refuelling trials held at the A&AEE, Boscombe Down, to enable the Hercules tanker to be quickly drafted into service during the Falklands campaign. (*Crown Copyright/Air Historical Branch image CNA-8273-3*)

The view from the cockpit of a Hercules as it positions to refuel behind Hercules C.1K XV201 in June 1994. The refuelling traffic lights are mounted on the rear of the tanker, and are just visible through the flexible basket. (*Crown Copyright/Air Historical Branch image DPR-792-61*)

While the speed of the Hercules tanker was occasionally a problem for some receiver aircraft, it proved fine for the Nimrod MR.2P. In this image taken during tanking trials with the A&AEE at Boscombe Down on 29 July 1982, Hercules C.1K XV201 was photographed refuelling Nimrod MR.2P XV254. (*Crown Copyright/Air Historical Branch image CNA-8324-10*)

ZD950 was the first Tristar KC.1 tanker/freighter conversion to undergo full conversion and was photographed during a flight test in 1985. Like all of the Tristar tanker conversions, it was fitted with twin FRL Mk 17R HDUs located in a special pressure cell in the rear fuselage and was photographed with one of the hose and collapsible drogue units deployed. (*Marshall's of Cambridge image MCE-35-2807-32*)

The production and assembly of the additional fuselage-mounted fuel tanks, taken during the conversion programme in 1984. (*Marshall's of Cambridge*)

Tristar KC.1 ZD950 undergoing refuelling trials in 1985 with Hercules C.1P XV210 acting as receiver. (*Marshall's of Cambridge*)

A No. 216 Squadron Tristar KC.1, ZD951, photographed while refuelling an unidentified Tornado F.3, while another Tornado F.3 looks on. (*Marshall's of Cambridge*)

No. 216 Squadron Tristar K.1 ZD948, now painted in the later grey colour scheme, was photographed while refuelling a pair of No. 3 Squadron Typhoon FGR.4 aircraft, including the specially painted ZJ936/QO-C. (*Marshall's of Cambridge*)

ZD948 was withdrawn from service and placed in storage at Bruntingthorpe on 25 March 2014 where it receives regular maintenance by GJD Services in anticipation of the aircraft being returned to the US. It was photographed at Bruntingthorpe on 28 July 2018. (*Keith Wilson*)

When the former civilian VC10 airliners were converted to military K.2 and K.3 tanker aircraft at Bristol, they were fitted with auxiliary fuel cells in the fuselage. These underwent significant testing at the factory ahead of installation. (*Keith Wilson*)

The first VC10 K.2 conversion was ZA141, which made its first flight in 1982 and appeared in this grey/green camouflage. During the acceptance trials at Boscombe Down, it underwent air-to-air refuelling trials with a number of receiver aircraft, including the Nimrod AEW.3 seen here refuelling from the centreline HDU. (*BAE Systems Image A6977 via Bristol Aero Collection Trust*)

VC10 K.2 ZA141/B, in its then-standard 'hemp' colour scheme, operating over the North Sea while refuelling a pair of No. 4 Squadron Harrier GR.7 aircraft – ZG856/CJ and ZG509/CH – in 1992. (*Keith Wilson*)

ZA148/G, a VC10 K.3 of No. 101 Squadron, refuelling a Hercules C.5 from its centreline HDU during a training exercise for the Hercules crew on 5 November 2008. At the time of the image, the Hercules was being operated by the A&AEE at Boscombe Down. (*Crown Copyright/Air Historical Branch image CCT-08-198-101/SAC Andy Holmes*)

All of the remaining VC10 C.1 aircraft were converted by Flight Refuelling Ltd at Hurn into C.1K tanker/transport aircraft. After conversion, the aircraft retained their No. 10 Squadron 'shiny' colour scheme, although they were painted in the regular 'grey' scheme later in their service life. XV109 was photographed while simultaneously refuelling a pair of Tornado F.3 aircraft – ZE339/FO from No. 25 Squadron at RAF Leeming (nearest the camera) and ZG780/BH from No. 29 Squadron at RAF Coningsby (farthest). (*Crown Copyright/Air Historical Branch image BZN-AAR-6*)

A pair of No. 2 Squadron Tornado GR.4As (ZA404/W and ZA400/T) were photographed while refuelling from a No. 101 Squadron VC10 K.2, ZA144, over the North Sea in April 1997. (*Crown Copyright/Air Historical Branch image DPR-876-38*)

No. 101 Squadron VC10 C.1K XV103 was photographed in 1994 while refuelling three Harrier GR.7 aircraft from No. 4 Squadron. Nearest the camera is the specially painted example ZG512, while the grey aircraft is ZD467/WA, which had just returned to No. 4 Squadron after a period on detachment at Incirlik, Turkey, during Operation Warden. (*Crown Copyright/Air Historical Branch image PHOTO-MIS-AAR-2*)

Wearing a No. 10 Squadron badge on its tail, VC10 C.1K XV107 was photographed during Exercise Eastern Smile in the Mediterranean on 30 June 2004. Two Typhoon T.1 aircraft (ZJ807/BF and ZJ806/BE) from No. 29 Squadron are taking on fuel while No. 31 Squadron Tornado GR.4 ZA563/DI awaits its turn. Exercise Eastern Smile involved an 8,000-mile journey to Singapore and for the two Typhoon aircraft represented their maiden tanking trail outside the UK. (*Crown Copyright/Air Historical Branch image AKR-04-228*)

Out with the old and in with the new. The last flight of VC10 K.3 ZA1560/J occurred on 24 September 2013, before it touched down at Dunsfold where the aircraft was to be preserved with the Brooklands Museum. The VC10 was joined in the air by No. 10 Squadron Voyager KC.2 ZZ331 for this very special photo shoot over the North Sea. (*Crown Copyright/Air Historical Branch image LEE-20130924-1142-009/Geoffrey Lee/Planefocus*)

Buddy-Buddy Tanking

Even the wide-angle lens used for this image cannot hide the close proximity of the two aircraft wh
taking on fuel during buddy-buddy tanking operations high over the North Sea on 3 December 1992. T
receiver is a No. 12 Squadron Buccaneer S.2, XX885, call sign 'Jackal 2', while another Buccaneer S.2B of t
same squadron (XW530, call sign 'K2P18') is providing the fuel. The refuelling sortie had been planned
low level over the sea but a build-up of cumulus nimbus clouds in the area meant the sortie was moved
into the smoother air at 18,000 feet, purely for the benefit of the civilian back-seater! (*Keith Wilson*)

The 'Buddy-Buddy' concept of air-to-air refuelling was primarily designed for fighter and bomb
aircraft where the hose-drum unit (HDU) and drogue, along with a suitable power supply, cou
be incorporated into an under-wing or under-fuselage 'drop tank'. It could be fitted to an aircr
in a relatively short time and permit them to operate as a tanker aircraft to other, similar aircr
It could also be removed relatively quickly to allow the aircraft to undertake its normal design
activities.

Interestingly, the concept of buddy-buddy tanking has been around almost as long as the idea
air-to-air refuelling itself! Back in April 1923, at Rockwell Field, San Diego, a pair of DH.4B aircr
of the US Army Air Corps took off with the intention of breaking the endurance record. The A/
method used was a development of one used by early barnstormers where the 'tanker' dangled
50-foot length of refuelling hose terminating in a trigger nozzle; which was grasped by the observ
of the 'receiver' and inserted into the open neck of the fuel filler, with fuel being transferred
gravity. Using this rather rudimentary method, the 'receiver' was able to remain aloft for 37 hou
and 15 minutes on 27/28 April. Sadly, what does not seem to have been recorded was the numb
of flight refuellings used to achieve the record. The event was given significant publicity and
encouraged others to experiment with similar trials on this side of the Atlantic.

Air-to-air refuelling developments continued apace but were largely linked to achieving or ~ating existing records for distance and endurance or, just before the Second World War, non-stop crossing of the Atlantic.

The Cold War brought about a significant change in the attitudes of the military minds. The ~S need to have missile-equipped bombers aloft 24/7, ready to attack or retaliate at a moment's ~tice, and have the range to get to and from the farthest targets required the benefit of air-to-air fuelling assets. Initially, the USAF adopted Flight Refuelling Limited's hose-and-drogue ~stem on their B-29 and B-50 tankers, but the need to refuel large aircraft in a minimum of ~ne required higher fuel flow rates than was previously available. Enter Boeing's 'Flying Boom' ~ethod of refuelling, later attached to the Boeing KC-135, which the USAF ordered in their ~ndreds.

However, in the UK, a paper written by C. H. Latimer-Needham, Chief Engineer of Flight ~efuelling, back in May 1951, recognised the absolute necessity of air-to-air refuelling if the UK's ~rce of nuclear deterrent Valiant bombers would even reach many of their required targets. ~entually, the military minds sat up and listened and the solution was a tanker converted from ~ Valiant bomber. The air-to-air refuelling trials conducted between Valiant B(PR)K.1s WZ376 ~d WZ390 in 1956 proved the concept and the RAF's first buddy-buddy tanking capability, ~beit with two very large aircraft!

Meanwhile, the USAF was pursuing something similar with their fleet of Boeing B-47 Stratojet ~x-engine nuclear strike-capable bombers, which saw service from 1951 through to 1965 with the ~rategic Air Command (SAC). This included 'Reflex' missions, a long-range and long-endurance ~ercise which saw the B-47 remain aloft for up to 18 hours while simulating bombing missions ~ainst Soviet targets. Against this background, two KB-47B aircraft were modified for flight ~sting of the UK-designed probe-and-drogue system and given the designation YB-47F, although ~ would later have been designated KB-47G. Other B-47 aircraft were used in the test programme ~ee picture on page 66) in what would have been an interesting buddy-buddy system. The tests ~ere being conducted around the same time that Boeing announced and tested its 'Model 80' ~ter KC-135) tanker, which provided better flexibility and a much greater fuel transfer rate. In ~54, the KB-47 programme was cancelled.

~S Navy Activities

~fter some RAF and USAF experimentation and testing, it was the naval arms of both countries ~at first saw the significant benefit of buddy-buddy tanking and put the system to good use. ~owadays, most, if not all, carrier-borne strike and attack aircraft are capable of launching from ~ catapult with a good head wind, with a full fuel and weapons load; but it wasn't always the ~se. Buddy-buddy tanking permitted the strike aircraft to get airborne with minimum fuel and ~aximum offensive armaments, before topping up with a tanker and heading off to the target.

The US Navy and Marine Corps embraced the tanker role, initially employing the North ~merican AJ-2 Savage aircraft to carry out those duties. It was followed on the US Navy aircraft ~rriers by the KA-3B Skywarrior, which was originally designed as a nuclear strike and attack ~rcraft but, when fitted with a probe-and-drogue refuelling system, proved very successful in ~is role while becoming very popular with its 'trade'. This was followed by the Douglas A-4B ~cyhawk in a pure buddy-buddy role, with the Grumman KA-6D Intruder later being introduced ~ replace the earlier KA-3B aircraft on aircraft carriers. This in turn was then replaced by the ~ckheed S-3 Viking as the US Navy's primary carrier-based tanker aircraft.

~Coming right up to date, the US Navy operates a fleet of Boeing F/A-18E/F Super Hornet ~rcraft as buddy-buddy 'Strike Tankers', which have taken over the role of the S-3 Vikings.

Royal Navy Buddy-Buddy Tanking

Having seen the progress being made in the US with the buddy-buddy tanking system durin a visit to Flight Refuelling Inc. in 1954, Sir Alan Cobham approached the Royal Air Force suggest how it could benefit the service. However, it was the Royal Navy that showed serio interest and was the first to operate the concept.

This was a self-contained ram air-turbine-powered pod that was easily attached or detach from the standard under-wing pylon of fighter and strike aircraft. The pod could be operated altitudes up to 45,000 feet, at operational airspeeds of 310 knots and carried in the non-operati condition up to 500 knots, or Mach 1.0. It would also possess the capability of being carri during an aircraft carrier launch and arrester landing. The proposed pod, later designated t Mk 20 by FRL, was 13 feet 7 inches in length, 28 inches in diameter and, apart from some sm. electrical requirements, was self-contained in power. It also had the capacity of 150 gallo (675 litres) of disposable fuel, and a transfer rate of 150 gallons (675 litres) per minute.

It was initially flown under the fuselage of Canberra WK143 with a Dowty-Rotol ten-blad constant-speed ram air turbine, to provide the 36 hp required to operate the fuel pump a hose-drum unit. Initially, it was fitted with a solid drogue similar to that used on the Valia tanker. This Mk 20 was fitted to the first Royal Navy Scimitar and Sea Vixen tankers whe they entered service in 1960. However, the shape of the pod was later streamlined and collapsible-type drogue added to the redesigned Mk 20A. It was an important design in the AA world and the Mk 20A became the pattern for many future buddy-buddy tanking options.

The need for shipboard tanking became apparent when the Buccaneer S.1 entered service wi the Royal Navy in 1961. The early Gyron Junior-powered Buccaneer S.1 aircraft did not posse sparkling performance. In fact, they could best be described as 'underpowered'. This becar apparent during the initial trials of the type aboard HMS *Victorious* in 1960 and, later, duri deck trials aboard HMS *Hermes* with No. 700Z Flight.

On 19 February 1963, No. 801 Squadron made its first deployment aboard HMS *Ark Roy* The underpowered Buccaneer S.1 was not always capable of getting airborne from the catap safely with a full offensive load as well as a full fuel load. The solution was to get the fully arm aircraft off the aircraft carrier and shortly afterwards fill it with fuel from a waiting tanker, order for the aircraft to be prepared for the mission. Thankfully, the Rolls-Royce Spey-power Buccaneer S.2 did not suffer in the same manner and was used for the buddy-buddy tanki role – equipped with a Mk 20 pod under the starboard wing and an auxiliary fuel slipper ta under the port wing – aboard the aircraft carriers.

However, the Scimitar, Sea Vixen and Buccaneer S.2 aircraft were all strike aircraft in the own right, as well as buddy-buddy capable, and were often used to refuel each other duri Royal Navy operations.

The benefit of buddy-buddy tanking to the Royal Navy was two-fold. In addition to providing safety cover over the aircraft carrier during poor-weather recoveries by enabling returning aircr to refuel while waiting for suitable weather before landing, it also provided a significant strateg benefit in that a tanker could rendezvous with attacking aircraft as they come off their first targ and refuel them before they could then attack a second target – effectively 'Force Multiplying'.

RAF Buddy-Buddy Capabilities

Soon after the Labour Government came into power in 1964, it signalled a remarkal change of fortunes for the Royal Navy. The political decision to phase out the use of aircr carriers eventually signalled an end to the Buccaneer S.2's service afloat. On 4 December 19

MS *Ark Royal*, the very last of the Royal Navy aircraft carriers, was withdrawn from service nd scrapped. Its aircraft were flown to RAF St Athan for disposal or reassignment to the RAF.

However, in July 1968, it had been decided to equip the RAF with the Buccaneer S.2, primarily) replace the F-111 aircraft, which in turn had been ordered to replace the cancelled TSR-2 roject. Although the RAF had not initially wanted the Buccaneer in their inventory, once 1 service it proved itself in a variety of roles, not least of which was the maritime strike)le. No. 12 Squadron was chosen as the first squadron to receive the Buccaneer S.2, when it eformed in October 1969. Initially based at RAF Honington, they moved to RAF Lossiemouth n 3 November 1980, effectively closer to its potential prey. Within No. 12 Squadron, and later o. 208 Squadron, the Buccaneer S.2's buddy-buddy capability was embraced and welcomed, roving to be of particular use during the training for the longer-range strike attack missions gainst enemy shipping the squadrons specialised in.

ornado Buddy-Buddy

Vhen the Buccaneer was withdrawn from service in March 1994, it was replaced in the maritime rike role by Sea Eagle-equipped Tornado GR.1B aircraft.

Trials with the RAF Tornado GR.1 aircraft equipped with a Mk 20G buddy-buddy refuelling ack had been undertaken following a request in January 1984 to provide refuelling capabilities) sixteen Tornado GR.1 aircraft. At the time, the option of the Sargent Fletcher 28-300 pod was lso available but the RAF favoured the FRL option of utilising surplus Mk 20B refuelling pods reviously in service with the Victor and Buccaneer fleet.

Despite the successful flight trials conducted with the A&AEE at Boscombe Down using ornado 'PO3' XX947 as a tanker and production Tornado 'PS15' XZ631 as the receiver, an order 'as not forthcoming. Interestingly, both the German Navy and Italian Air Force did see the enefits of buddy-buddy tanking but ordered the Sargent Fletcher 28-300 pod equipment for leir use. That said, it has been reported that Sargent Fletcher 28-300 pods were acquired by the AF during the Gulf War in 1991 but not used.

Later, in August 1993, a further study was undertaken for the equipping of up to twenty-four ornado GR.1 aircraft with buddy-buddy tanker capabilities by scavenging FRL Mk 20 pods from 'ictor K.2 aircraft that were due to be withdrawn from service shortly afterwards. The plan was to ave the aircraft in service by 1996–7 and spread around all of the Tornado GR.1 units. The rationale ehind the conversion was to supplement the RAF's main tanker force, which was being stretched) its limits by operational commitments. Sadly, the plan did not lead to an order being placed.

uddy-Buddy Tanker Across the Globe

he application is not limited to the forces of the US and the UK. The French Air Force saw 1e benefits when operating their Dassault Mirage IV supersonic strategic bomber aircraft, an nportant part of France's nuclear deterrent which often operated in a pair with the second ircraft being the tanker. Meanwhile, the Aeronavale operated Dassault-Breguet Super Étendard nd Dassault Rafale aircraft in the buddy-buddy role.

The Soviet Air Force had started buddy-buddy trials in the mid-1970s, using Sukhoi u-15 Flagons with a centre-line-mounted hose/drogue pod. It is believed that this did not rogress to operational use but was to establish the parameters of buddy-buddy refuelling for 1e Su-24. It later operated the Sukhoi Su-24MK Fencer-D equipped with the UPAZ-1A (UPAZ – Inified Refuelling Pod) Sakhalin buddy-buddy tanker pod on the underside of the fuselage in ddition to a pair of 3,000-litre under-wing-mounted auxiliary fuel tanks. The plan was to be able to refuel both Su-24s and Mikoyan MiG-3 Foxhound interceptors. In addition, a number of Mikoyan MiG-29K and Tupolev Tu-16N aircraft were also modified for the buddy-buddy role.

The Soviet Navy operated up to twenty-four Sukhoi Su-33 Flanker-D aircraft, including many aboard the aircraft carrier *Admiral Kuznetsov*. Some of these Su-33M aircraft operated in the buddy-buddy tanking role.

Cobham developed the 754 Buddy Store for use by the Indian Air Force on their Sukhoi Su-30 aircraft, providing a refuelling flow rate of up to 410 US gallons (1,552 litres) per minute for the aircraft. In addition, the Su-30 aircraft of the Malaysian Air Force have been similarly equipped.

Following the purchase of a pair of FRL Mk XIV hose drum units for flight trials with the USAF, one was installed into the rear fuselage of a Boeing B-47B while the other was fitted into a Convair B-36 that was also equipped with a retractable boom through which the refuelling hose was trailed. This image shows refuelling trials with a B-47 aircraft suitably modified with an air-to-air receiving probe. Both trials were ultimately successful but the Boeing boom was accepted for operational use within the USAF. (*Cobham plc*)

Although the RAF was approached by FRL with regard to the buddy-buddy tanking capability, it was the Royal Navy who first operated the concept. Utilising the FRL Mk 20 pod under the starboard wing, along with an additional long-range fuel tank under the starboard wing, trials were conducted by de Havilland Hatfield using a pair of RN Sea Vixen FAW.1 aircraft (XJ488 and XJ521). This image was taken during those trials on 23 February 1960. (*de Havilland Aircraft Company image 12703A via BAE Systems*)

The original FRL Mk 20 refuelling pod was fitted to a Sea Vixen FAW.1 at Hatfield on 28 April 1960. In this early iteration the pod featured a ten-blade constant-speed ram air turbine on the front and a solid drogue to the rear. It was later modified with a two-blade ram air turbine and collapsible-type drogue and was designated the Mk 20A. (*de Havilland Aircraft Company image 12799A via BAE Systems*)

In the early 1960s, the Royal Navy took part in a refuelling interchange with the US Navy, having introduced the Mk 8 reception coupling and probe nozzle. To demonstrate the flexibility of the probe and drogue system, four aircraft linked up in line astern, making contact with the aircraft in front. The trial was led by a RN Sea Vixen, followed by a US Navy A-4 Skyhawk and an A-3 Skywarrior, with a RN Scimitar completing the line. (*Crown Copyright/Air Historical Branch image A&AEE-AAR-1*)

In January 1963, a design study was conducted by FRL and the Armstrong Whitworth Division of Hawker Siddeley Aviation for the conversion of the Argosy C.1 freighter aircraft into a tanker and receiver. The proposal featured a modified Mk 20 refuelling pod (designated Mk 20D) along with four standard overload fuel tanks installed in the tanker's fuselage, offering a total of 1,720 gallons of fuel available for pumping. Two aircraft were involved in the trials conducted by the A&AEE at Boscombe Down (XN814 as the tanker and XN816 as the receiver), which were completed satisfactorily. However, no further aircraft were modified and the project was cancelled. (*Crown Copyright/Air Historical Branch image A&AEE-936-1*)

The trials Buccaneer S.2 XN975, fitted with a FRL Mk 20 refuelling pod under its starboard wing, along with an additional fuel slipper tank fitted under the port wing; it is photographed while providing fuel to a No. 700 NAS Buccaneer S.1, XN923, during manufacturer's buddy-buddy tanking trials on 4 April 1965. (*BAE Systems Image BAL20828*) (*BAE Systems Image BAL2082945*)

A No. 12 Squadron Buccaneer S.2B, XW530 (callsign 'K2P18'), operating in the buddy-buddy tanker fit, with the FRL Mk 20C refuelling pod installed under the starboard wing and an addition slipper tank fitted beneath the port wing. The hose and drogue have been trailed, awaiting the first receiver. (*Keith Wilson*)

High over the North Sea in December 1992, the first receiver for fuel is another No. 12 Squadron Buccaneer S.2B, XW527 (call sign 'Jackal 1'), who positions on the starboard side of the tanker before being cleared onto the hose. (*Keith Wilson*)

Once cleared to do so, the receiver can move forward onto the basket and, after pushing the hose forward, the fuel flows. XW527 ('Jackal 1') is seen receiving fuel in this image. (*Keith Wilson*)

With XW527 ('Jackal 1') and XZ431 ('Jackal 4') having received their allotted fuel, XV332 ('Jackal 3') takes his turn to refuel from XW530. This image was taken from inside XX885 ('Jackal 2'), who then took his turn on the hose. Once all four aircraft had been refuelled, 'Jackal Formation' continued their sortie. (*Keith Wilson*)

When the military forces of Argentina invaded the Falkland Islands on 1 April 1982, the RAF's main transport aircraft – the Hercules C.1 – was not capable of flying the 3,900-mile distance from Ascension Island to Port Stanley without in-flight refuelling. Hastily, a contract was given to Marshall Engineering to install the necessary probes to the fleet, enabling the aircraft to support the task force. Later, six Hercules aircraft were also modified by Marshall Engineering to become single-point tankers, with the addition of a FRL Mk 17B HDU; the entire package was mounted onto the upper rear cargo ramp. Here, a Hercules C.1K, XV204, was photographed while refuelling Hercules C.1P XV210 over the Bristol Channel during a tanker training sortie from RAF Lyneham. (*Keith Wilson*)

In August 1993, a plan was considered to re-use the Mk 20B HDUs from eight surplus Victor K.2 aircraft of No. 55 Squadron that were due to be withdrawn from use on 1 October 1993. The plan was to add a reworked Mk 20G refuelling pod to the underside of the Tornado GR.1 fuselage and then spread the buddy-buddy-capable Tornado fleet throughout the Service's GR.1 squadrons. Although the design work was undertaken by FRL and tested at Boscombe Down, the capability was never ordered. In this image, taken during refuelling trails at Boscombe Down, pre-production Tornado 'PS15' XZ631 was photographed being refuelled by Tornado 'PO3' XX947 using the modified FRL Mk 20G refuelling pod. (*BAE Systems Image AWCN22690*)

Buddy-buddy tanking on a large scale! A No. 101 Squadron VC10 K.3, ZA149/H, refuels a VC.10 C.1K, XV104/U, using the centreline FRL Mk 17B HDU, high over the North Sea. (*Crown Copyright/Air Historical Branch image 'Tanking the tanker'*)

The US Navy saw the benefits of buddy-buddy tanking very early in its development and have been keen proponents of the capability ever since. Here, a US Navy F/A-18F (coded NF-106) was photographed while refuelling a similar F/A-18E (coded NF-202) using the Cobham 31-300 series refuelling pod. (*Cobham plc*)

The A330 Voyager MRTT

330 MRTT Voyager KC.2 ZZ331 from No. 10 Squadron at RAF Brize Norton simultaneously refuels rnado GR.4 ZG775/134 from No. 617 Squadron at Marham and Typhoon FGR.4 ZK342/ED from No. 6 quadron at Leuchars. (*Crown Copyright/Air Historical Branch image GHL-139796/Geoffrey Lee/Planefocus*)

he Airbus A330 Multi Role Tanker Transport (MRTT) is a fourth-generation aerial refuelling nker and transport aircraft based on the civilian A330-200 airliner. From the outset, it was esigned as a dual-role air-to-air refuelling platform and can be equipped with a combination of pecialist AAR equipment, making it an attractive proposition to a number of air arms across ie globe.

Firstly, it was designed to carry the Cobham 905E under-wing refuelling pods for the refuelling ⸍ probe-equipped receiver aircraft – especially fast jets such as the Typhoon and Tornado – hile operating as a two-point tanker. The 905E wing pod can deliver fuel at a rate of up to 50 US gallons per minute, delivering fuel from a hose up to 90 feet in length, within a speed inge of 185 to 350 knots. It can also refuel two aircraft simultaneously, effectively delivering p to 900 US gallons a minute.

In addition, the A330 MRTT can also be fitted with a Cobham 805E Fuselage Refuelling Unit RU) for probe-equipped receivers – now operating as a three-point tanker. With a fuel flow ite of up to 700 US gallons per minute, from an 85-foot trailed hose, the 805E is eminently iitable for the refuelling of larger aircraft.

Finally, from a tanker perspective, the A330MRTT can also be fitted with the Airbus Military erial Refuelling Boom System (ARBS) – very similar to the Boeing flying boom system and iitable for all receptacle-equipped aircraft. The ability for the aircraft to refuel a variety of receiver type makes the A330MRTT a truly flexible tanker asset. The Airbus ARBS permits t. fastest possible fuel transfer rate currently available, which reduces the time required for a refuelling operation – all at altitudes up to 35,000 feet and at speeds from 180 to 350 knots.

Finally, as a receiver, it can be fitted with a Universal Aerial Refuelling Receptacle Slipw Installation (UARRSI), enabling it to be refuelled in flight from another tanker's boom.

Capacities and Capabilities

The Airbus A330-200 wing is large enough to hold all of the fuel required in the tanking ro without requiring the installation of additional fuel cells and thereby avoiding any reduction its ability to carry passengers or cargo.

Able to refuel any receiver, the A330MRTT can carry up to 111 tonnes (245,000 lbs) of fuel its tanks. In a deployment mission, the A330MRTT enables four Eurofighter Typhoon aircra to fly up to 3,600 n.m. (5,794 km); or, when carrying up to 20 tonnes (44,800 lbs) of payload, deploy four fighters a distance of 2,800 n.m. (4,500 km).

When used on 'towline' missions, such as those conducted around the shores of the UK on daily basis, it can be on station at around 1,000 n.m. (1,600 km) from its base for up to 4 hou and 30 minutes, with the ability to provide up to 50 tonnes of fuel to receivers. Or it can provi 60 tonnes of fuel to receivers while on station for up to 5 hours at 500 n.m. (800 km) from bas This performance exceeds anything any other current tanker can operate.

With its widebody fuselage design, the A330MRTT is able to carry a wide range of milita or humanitarian payloads on strategic missions. It can carry a payload of up to 45 tonn (99,000 lbs) and the cargo can be carried under the floor in any of the standard civilian containe and pallets, as well as the standard 88 x 108-inch Model 463L NATO military pallets. The ma deck can also be used for cargo when the aircraft is configured as a freighter. Furthermore, t aircraft can also be configured to operate in a 'combi' mode, to carry freight in the forward pa of the main deck and passengers/troops in the aft section. In a single-class configuration, t A330MRTT cabin can be modified to carry up to 380 passengers, allowing a complete range configurations from maximised troop transport to complex customisation suitable for VIP a guest missions. Finally, the A330MRTT can also be used for medical evacuation (MEDIVAC), its cabin can easily be converted to accommodate up to 130 stretchers.

Production and Deliveries

Standard Airbus A330-200 aircraft are delivered from the Airbus Final Assembly line in Toulou to the Airbus Military Conversion Centre in Getafe, Spain, for the installation of the require refuelling systems, along with the military avionics and control systems. The A330MRTT manufactured to conform to the latest civil aviation requirements and was certified by t Spanish authorities in October 2010.

The A330 MRTT's wing has a common structure with the four-engine Airbus A340-20 and -300, with reinforced mounting locations and the provision of fuel piping for the A34C outboard engines. Consequently, the A330MRTT's wing required little modification for use these hardpoints for the fitting of the under-wing-mounted refuelling pods.

Australia was the launch customer for the A330MRTT, with the first delivery made to the Roy Australian Air Force (RAAF) on 1 June 2011. However, the remaining four aircraft delivered to t RAAF were converted by Qantas Defence Services at its Brisbane Airport facility on behalf of EAD

Aside from the RAAF and the RAF, the A330MRTT has also been ordered by the United Emirat Air Force, the Royal Saudi Air Force, the Republic of Singapore Air Force, the South Korea

Force and the French Air Force, although the exact number of aircraft to be delivered to the ter remains undecided due to political issues.

The EADS/Northrop Grumman KC-45 was a version of the A330MRTT proposed for the United ates Air Force and if the political 'influences' in the US had remained outside of the military ding and selection process, the type may already be in service with the USAF.

In 2002, when the USAF ran a procurement process to replace around 100 of their oldest C-135E Stratotankers, EADS offered the A330MRTT. The Boeing KC-767 was selected but the ntract was cancelled when it was discovered that illegal manipulation and corrupt practices d apparently taken place during the competition. A similar process was held in 2006 and 2007, s time to replace the entire KC-135 fleet. Proposed by EADS and Northrop Grumman as the C-30, it again competed against the Boeing 767, which is a smaller aircraft, holding around 20 r cent less fuel, less cargo, but was cheaper. In 2008, it was announced that the winner was the C-30, later re-designated the KC-45A.

Sadly, and not for the first time, having not got the desired answer to their question on the cond bidding process, the politicians appealed the decision to the Government Accountability ffice (GAO). Somewhat unsurprisingly, Boeing's appeal was upheld and the USAF was forced re-bid the entire process. In 2009, the parameters were apparently re-written and the Boeing C-46 was the eventually winner at the third (and final) attempt!

ultinational Multi-Role Tanker Transport Fleet

November 2011, the European Defence Agency (EDA) Steering Board and European defence inisters endorsed air-to-air refuelling (AAR) as one of the initial Pooling and Sharing itiatives, having recognised the need for a greater AAR capability. Up to this point, there had en a near-constant reliance on USAF tanker aircraft during the military intervention in Libya ring 2011. A letter of intent was signed by the defence ministers of ten EDA member states the llowing year, for the procurement of a new Multi-Role Tanker Transport Fleet (MMF) project. ith the usual speed and procrastination expected of the European Union, it was not until 2017 en a 'final' decision was made with an order for eight aircraft being placed with Airbus for e A330MRTT – with five expected to be operated from Eindhoven air base and the remaining ree at Koln-Bonn air base.

AF Acquisition by Private Finance Initiative

ack in January 2004, the Ministry of Defence (MoD) announced that a variant of the A330MRTT d been selected to provide the tanking capability for the RAF for the next thirty years under e Future Strategic Tanker Aircraft (FSTA) Programme. The new type would replace all tanking sets then in RAF service: the VC10 and Tristar fleets normally based at RAF Brize Norton.

On 27 March 2008, the MoD signed an agreement to lease fourteen aircraft under a Private nance Initiative arrangement with the EADS-led consortium AirTanker. Two versions were to ordered: the Voyager KC.2 with a pair of under-wing-mounted Cobham 905E refuelling pods ted as a two-point tanker; and the Voyager KC.3, which also featured a Cobham 805E Fuselage fuelling Unit (FRU) in addition to the wing pods, as a three-point tanker. Both versions were be powered by Rolls-Royce Trent 772B-60 engines of 71,100 lb st (316 kN).

By May 2014 ten aircraft had been delivered, representing the 'core fleet' of RAF aircraft. e remaining four aircraft were 'surge capability': available to the RAF if and when required t otherwise available to AirTanker – to quote the terms of the agreement – for tasks such 'release to the civil market, less its military equipment or to partner nations in a military capacity with the MoD's agreement'. By 14 March 2016, all fourteen Voyager aircraft had be 'delivered' to the RAF, although four of these aircraft remain on the UK civil aircraft register

Into Service

In RAF service, the Voyager had particularly big boots to fill! Both the Tristar and VC10 h served the RAF well, especially the VC10 in theatre. The Tristar was an excellent strategic tank with its combined tanker/transport capabilities and had also served in theatre in both Gulf Wa

The VC10 was a popular tactical tanker, especially with fast jet crews in theatre, and provid sterling service during Operations Granby (first Gulf war), Warden (Iraq), Allied Force (Kosov Veritas (Afghanistan), Herrick (Afghanistan), Telic (second Gulf war) and Ellamy (milita intervention in Libya), where it was also popular with both US Navy and US Marine Cor fast jet receivers. However, the troop-carrying and medivac capabilities of the VC10 C.1K a K.4 variants should not be forgotten.

Voyager is now the RAF's sole air-to-air refuelling tanker, while it also operates as a strateg air transport aircraft – operating at RAF Brize Norton with both Nos 10 and 101 Squadron Under the terms of the Private Finance Initiative, AirTanker owns, manages and maintai the aircraft while providing infrastructure support, training facilities and some personnel, particular Sponsored Reserve pilots and engineers.

The first Voyager in service began operations with No. 10 Squadron on 12 May 2012, flying air transport sortie into RAF Akrotiri. Issues with the drogues during early refuelling operatio delayed the Voyager's debut in the tanker role, but these had been overcome by the summer 2013 and the aircraft's ability to deliver fuel to a variety of RAF and allied aircraft expand rapidly. In the same year, No. 101 Squadron retired the RAF's final VC10 tanker aircraft a began operating the Voyager alongside No. 10 Squadron and AirTanker reservists.

In addition to the aircraft based at RAF Brize Norton, one aircraft is always available the Falkland Islands, primarily in support of the Typhoon QRA jets, but also available to t Hercules fleet. Another Voyager operates the regular airbridge to and from the Falklands.

In Theatre

Since its introduction into service, the Voyager has been making a significant contribution Operation Shader, where the aircraft provides air-to-air refuelling capabilities to RAF Torna and Typhoon aircraft, as well as a variety of coalition jets, including US Marine Corps Harri and F/A-18 Hornet aircraft.

Serials and Models

The following Voyager aircraft operate under the terms of the AirTanker agreement:

Serial	Type Designation	Delivery Date	Former/current civil identity
ZZ330	Voyager KC.2	21 December 2011	Ex G-VYGA
ZZ331	Voyager KC.2	19 December 2011	Ex G-VYGB
ZZ332	Voyager KC.3	26 April 2013	Ex G-VYGC
ZZ333	Voyager KC.3	29 May 2013	Ex G-VYGD
ZZ334	Voyager KC.3	31 July 2014	Ex G-VYGE
ZZ335	Voyager KC.3	29 June 2013	Ex G-VYGF
ZZ336	Voyager KC.3	30 November 2013	Ex G-VYGG
ZZ337	Voyager KC.3	29 January 2014	Ex G-VYGH

.338	Voyager KC.3	29 May 2014	Ex G-VYGI
.339	Airbus A330-243	14 August 2014	To G-VYGJ
.340	Airbus A330-243	5 February 2015	To G-VYGK
.341	Airbus A330-243	22 June 2015	To G-VYGL
.342	Airbus A330-243	24 February 2016	To G-VYGM
.343	Voyager KC.2	13 July 2016	Ex G-VYGN

(information from UK Serials Resource Centre, www.ukserials.com)

...ying Boom Under Consideration for RAF

...l of the Voyager aircraft delivered to the RAF are either two- or three-point tankers utilising ...e Cobham hose and drogue service. The lack of ARBS prevents them from being able to refuel ...number of types within the RAF inventory, including the C-17 Globemaster, E-3D Sentry and ...-135W, along with the proposed P-8 Poseidon.

...In April 2016, the RAF indicated an interest in the idea of fitting ARBS to a few of the Voyager ...et, bringing the aircraft in line with other A330MRTT operators around the world. The fitting ...the boom would permit the air-to-air refuelling of not only the aircraft mentioned above, but ...large number of other types in both the NATO and USAF inventory. At the time of writing, ... decision appears to have been reached.

...rbus A330 MRTT Voyager
...C.2 ' MRTT016' undergoing
...-to-air refuelling trails with
...phoon T.1 ZJ699, which was
...erated as a trials aircraft
... BAE Systems at Warton.
...RTT016' later entered
...AF service in May 2012 as
...330. (*QinetiQ Ltd via Airbus
...fence and Space*)

...e 'glass' cockpit interior of
...oyager KC.2 ZZ330 at Brize
...orton on 12 May 2012, ahead
... its first trooping flight into
...AF Akrotiri, Cyprus. (*Crown
...opyright/Air Historical Branch
...age MNT-20120512-078-099/
...C Ben Lees*)

An F-35B trials aircraft marked as 'BF-04' undergoing an air-to-air refuelling test flight on 26 April 2016 while being flown by RAF Squadron Leader Andy Edgell. The tanker is an RAF Voyager KC.3, ZZ334. (*Lockheed Martin via Cobham plc*)

The view from the left-hand seat of an RAF Hercules C.4 as it approaches a Voyager KC.3 tanker during a refuelling test flight on 18 December 2015. (*Dickie Allen via Airbus Defence and Space*)

The view from the back seat of a No. 29(R) Squadron Typhoon T.1 as it moves in to refuel from the starboard HDU aboard Voyager KC.3 ZZ335 on 22 June 2015 during a training sortie. (*Crown Copyright/Air Historical Branch image CON-20150622-0995-052/SAC Hannah Beavers*)

On 15 October 2014, No. 41 Squadron Tornado GR.4 ZA614/EB-Z was undertaking a missile test-firing over the Atlantic Ocean. During the sortie, which was supported by a Voyager KC.3, ZZ335, providing air-to-air refuelling, the Tornado successfully fired four Storm Shadow missiles. In addition to its regular squadron duties, No. 41 Squadron also serves as the RAF's Test and Evaluation Squadron (TES) from its base at RAF Coningsby. (*Crown Copyright/Air Historical Branch image LEE-20141015-1224-087/Cpl Mark Parkinson*)

On 1 July 2014, an RAF Airbus A330 MRTT marked as 'MRTT016' provided tanking facilities for refuelling trials with an Airbus A400M. The A400M can be fitted with a nose probe which can be removed when not required. The A400M can also be converted into an air refuelling tanker, an option which may be available to the RAF, who currently operate a fleet of twenty aircraft (with two more on order), with the type already in service at RAF Brize Norton, with Nos LXX, 24 and 206 Squadrons. (*Airbus Defence and Space image DSCN2233*)

The RAF's tenth Airbus MRTT, a Voyager KC.3, ZZ334, in AirTanker markings and equipped with a pair of Cobham 905E under-wing refuelling pods visible in this image, was photographed arriving at RAF Brize Norton on 14 August 2014. (*Crown Copyright/Air Historical Branch image BZN-20140814-842-001/Paul Crouch*)

An excellent close-up view of one of the RAF's latest F-35B Lightning aircraft, photographed while taking on fuel from an RAF Voyager tanker during the delivery flight from the USA on 3 August 2018. (*Crown Copyright/Air Historical Branch image 7644-20180803-027/Fg Off Paul Gale*)

A pair of No. 617 Squadron F-35B Lightning aircraft (ZM146 and ZM147) photographed while taking on fuel from Voyager KC.3 ZZ334 high over the North Sea on 27 November 2018 during Exercise Point Blank, the very first exercise that the new RAF F-35 aircraft have participated in. (*Crown Copyright/Air Historical Branch image LEE-OFFICIAL-20181127-886/Alex Scott*)

A No. 9 Squadron Tornado GR.4, normally based at RAF Marham in Norfolk, was photographed while refuelling from a Voyager KC.2 during Operation Shader on 22 October 2015 over Northern Iraq. The Tornado was based at RAF Akrotiri as part of the Tornado Detachment (TORDET) which operated within the 83 EAG (Expeditionary Air Group). (*Crown Copyright/Air Historical Branch image AUAB-20151022-138-300/Cpl Alex Scott*)

Air-to-air refuelling was first employed in theatre by the United States Air Force during the Korean War, utilising British-designed and manufactured hose-and-drogue technology on specially modified Boeing KB-29M and later KB-50J tanker aircraft. Some of the earliest refuelling sorties involved USAF F-80 and F-84 jet fighters utilising some of the earliest Sargent Fletcher tip tank probes. This required each aircraft to refuel both tip tanks separately, without the benefit of cross-feeding the tanks. That said, AAR had a major influence on the capability of the aircraft involved.

Seeing the benefits of AAR, the US Navy were quick to follow suit and employed medium-sized tankers like the single-point Grumman Panther before taking delivery of the first of six giant four-point Convair R3Y-2 Tradewind tankers. In September 1956, an R3Y-2 became the first tanker to simultaneously refuel four aircraft in flight, when four Grumman F9F Cougars were the receivers. Sadly, the programme was halted after thirteen R3Y-2 aircraft had been constructed following the unreliability of the Allison T-40 turboprop engines.

Having seen the benefits of AAR, the US Navy continued to develop smaller buddy-buddy tanking operations; with aircraft such as the KA-3B and EKA-3B Skywarrior tanker conversion used during the Vietnam War, Douglas A-4 Skyhawk aircraft were equipped for buddy-buddy tanking and Grumman KA-6D Intruder dedicated tanker all played an important role in future US Naval operations.

Nuclear Deterrent Drives the Demand for Tankers

With the development of Boeing's flying boom for the USAF, along with the development of the KC-97L and KC-135 for the US Air Force – driven largely by the Cold War requirement of th

82

US to be able to keep fleets of nuclear–armed B-47 Stratojet and B-52 Stratofortress strategic bombers airborne, both as a retaliatory threat against the Soviet Union or as an around-the-clock nuclear deterrent – the need to have suitable tankers aloft with the ability to deliver large quantities of jet fuel in as short a time as possible saw the flying boom come into its own. Able to deliver fuel at a significantly higher flow rate, while at the same time de-skilling the AAR process for the receiver, the USAF went down the Boeing-designed AAR route.

Aside from the nuclear deterrent role, the large quantity of flying-boom-equipped KC-135A aircraft were soon able to demonstrate their ability during the Vietnam War, with large numbers of aircraft being supported in theatre by the tankers – but in particular, the F-105 Thunderchiefs and F-4 Phantoms. It was during the Vietnam War that tanker support really came of age and proved its worth.

UK Tanking Requirements Driven by Nuclear Deterrent

As early as May 1951, C. H. Latimer-Needham, then the Chief Engineer of Flight Refuelling, clearly identified the 'Force Multiplier' impact of AAR during a design study that was presented to the Air Ministry in the strictest of secrecy! It identified the absolute need for a tanker force to support the new V-Bomber Force – and in particular the 'new' Valiant B.1 aircraft – with a real opportunity of striking all of the essential targets in the Soviet Union, if the need should ever arise. As a direct result of the study, Vickers were tasked, with the assistance of Flight Refuelling Limited, to convert a number of Valiant aircraft into AAR tankers, along with others capable of being in-flight refuelled. Once in service, the Valiant bombers were not just capable of refuelling the Valiant bomber fleet but any fighter, cargo or transport aircraft suitably modified with a probe to receive fuel in flight.

Thankfully, the need never arose for the nuclear deterrent aircraft to demonstrate their ability. However, the capability of AAR was firmly instilled into the planners and operators in the RAF, as well as the Royal Navy. While numerous trials were conducted, the practice of AAR was conducted almost daily somewhere around the UK. The system was not tested by the RAF in theatre until the 1982 Falklands War, where the recovery of the islands would not have been possible without AAR.

The following are the conflicts in which the RAF has employed air-to-air refuelling capabilities in theatre, along with details of the types of tankers used:

Operation Corporate

On 2 April 1982, Argentina invaded the Falkland Islands and the British Government, led by Margaret Thatcher, resolved to recapture them. Operate Corporate was the name given to the RAF's involvement in the recovery process. Up until then, British defence planning had been firmly focused on the Cold War.

The nearest airfield available to the RAF for their operations was on Ascension Island – with a single 10,000-foot runway – which lay almost 3,700 miles from the UK. Furthermore, the Falkland Islands were located a further 3,300 miles further away. As a consequence, air-to-air refuelling had a major contribution to play in the conflict.

At the time, the RAF had just twenty-three tanker aircraft in its inventory – all Victor K.2 aircraft operated by Nos 55 and 57 Squadrons at RAF Marham – which at the time were primarily engaged in the air defence of the UK. On 18 April, the first of the Victor K.2 aircraft were deployed to Ascension Island, where some were modified for the radar reconnaissance role which they flew on the night of 20/21 April, supported by four further Victor K.2 tanker aircraft in each direction. At the height of operations, fourteen Victor K.2 aircraft were based at Ascension Island.

The distance between Ascension and Port Stanley made re-supply very difficult. As a result a number of Hercules C.1 aircraft were hastily modified by Marshall's of Cambridge into C.1K aircraft following the fitting of an air-to-air receiving probe along with the necessary plumbing and, by using Victor K.2 tanker aircraft, were able to make the round trip. Similarly, six Vulcan bombers were similarly modified as receivers in record time. All six had been selected as they had the slightly higher power of the Bristol Olympus 301 fitted; the extra power would be absolutely essential when lifting a fully loaded and fuelled Vulcan from the runway at Ascension Island.

The tanking operations fell firmly on the shoulders of Nos 55 and 57 Squadrons, who between them flew more than 3,000 hours in 600 sorties with only six missions aborted through equipment failure.

As a result of the lack of AAR assets during this conflict, plans were put into place to modify six surplus Vulcan B.2 bombers into tankers while a contract was placed with Marshall's of Cambridge to convert six Hercules C.1 aircraft into single-point tankers. However, all were delivered too late for an active role in this conflict.

The Falklands War lasted just seventy-four days, with the Argentine forces surrendering on 14 June 1982.

Operation Black Buck (1–7)

During the 1982 Falklands War a series of seven very long-range missions by Vulcan B.2 aircraft selected from the Waddington Wing – comprising Nos 44, 50 and 101 Squadrons – was planned against Argentine forces occupying the Falkland Islands. These sorties were given the code names Black Buck 1 to Black Buck 7. Five of the planned seven raids were completed successfully.

At almost 6,800 nautical miles and lasting up to 16 hours for the journey from and returning to Ascension Island, they were the longest-ranged bombing raids in history. Each raid also required one of the most complex air-to-air refuelling plans ever created and it is a credit to all of the crews involved that they were all conducted safely and without loss of life.

Black Buck 1 was launched from Ascension Island on 1 May 1982 and involved a single Vulcan B.2 aircraft (XM607) attacking Port Stanley. Twenty-one 1,000 lb bombs were dropped from 10,000 feet across the runway, which was cratered by one bomb while others caused damage to aircraft and installations. Black Buck 1 involved a round-trip of 14 hours and 50 minutes for the crew of the Vulcan and required fifteen Victor K.2 tanker sorties and eighteen in-flight refuelling contacts to get the single aircraft to the target.

Details of the Black Buck missions are as follows:

Mission	Target	Date	Primary Vulcan	Secondary Vulcan	Notes
Black Buck 1	Port Stanley Airport runway	30 April – 1 May	XM598	XM607	Performed by reserve
Black Buck 2	Port Stanley Airport runway	3–4 May	XM607	XM598	Performed by primary
Black Buck 3	Port Stanley Airport runway	13 May	XM607	XM612	Cancelled due to weather

Black Buck 4	Anti-aircraft Radar	28 May	XM597	XM598	Cancelled due to tanker
Black Buck 5	Anti-aircraft Radar	31 May	XM597	XM598	Performed by primary
Black Buck 6	Anti-aircraft Radar	3 June	XM597	XM598	Performed but diverted to Brazil due to a broken refuelling probe
Black Buck 7	Port Stanley Airport stores and aircraft	12 June	XM607	XM598	Performed by primary

Operation Granby

Operation Granby was the name given to British military operations during the 1991 Gulf War. The build-up to the conflict had started earlier when the decision was made to deploy British forces to the Gulf. In August 1990, No. 5 Squadron deployed their Tornado F.3 aircraft to Dharan while No. 6 Squadron deployed their Jaguar GR.1A aircraft to Thumrait, all with the support of No. 101 Squadron VC10 tanker aircraft. Later, VC10s were co-located at Thumrait to support the Jaguars; however, the base proved unsuitable for the VC10 operations and they were moved to Seeb.

The first part of the Gulf War was directed at the Iraqi Air Force and its infrastructure. RAF Tornado aircraft were involved in strike missions, supported by No. 101 Squadron VC10 K.2 and K.3 tankers.

During the conflict, all nine VC10 K.2 and K.3 aircraft of No. 101 Squadron were deployed to bases in Bahrain, Saudi Arabia and Oman as part of Operation Granby. During the seven-month period No. 101 Squadron was deployed, they achieved a sortie success rate of over 99 per cent, flying 981 sorties involving 3,650 hours, while offloading 22,800 tonnes of fuel.

Two Tristar aircraft were deployed to King Khalid International Airport, near Riyadh in Saudi Arabia, where they operated as tankers, with the remainder of the Tristar fleet being utilised as transport aircraft between the Persian Gulf and the UK. The two Tristar aircraft were both painted in a special 'Desert Pink' colour scheme, earning the unfortunate nickname 'The Pink Pig'!

Operation Warden

Following the first Gulf War, and in order to protect the Kurds in the north of Iraq from further hostilities at the hands of the Iraqi Forces, a 'No Fly Zone' (NFZ) was mandated by the United Nations which effectively prevented the Iraqi army and air force from operating any aircraft north of the 36th Parallel. RAF Jaguar and Harrier GR.7 aircraft were deployed to the Turkish air force base at Incirlik under Operation Warden. Later, Tornado aircraft assumed responsibility for this operation. Initial tanker support was provided by a No. 55 Squadron K.2 aircraft operating from Incirlik but this was supplemented and later replaced by a VC10 K.2 or K.3 aircraft from No. 101 Squadron, which also operated from the Turkish base at Incirlik.

Operation Jural

By mid-1992, it became apparent that a similar NFZ arrangement was required to protect the Shi'ite Arabs in southern Iraq from Iraqi government forces. A small force of RAF Tornado GR.1A reconnaissance aircraft was employed in the low-level role in a similar manner to which they ha been during the Gulf War. They were used to gather intelligence about, and to monitor, the Iraq ground forces, while the US and French fighter aircraft prevented Iraqi Air Force aircraft from flying south of the 32nd Parallel. The US/Coalition operation was known as Southern Watch, and th British participation was given the name Operation Jural. Six Tornado GR.1A aircraft were deploye to Dharan while a single Victor K.2 from No. 55 Squadron was also deployed here for AAR suppor

Operation Ingleton

Although the daily reconnaissance tasks for the Tornado GR.1A aircraft involved in Operatio Jural had become routine by mid-December, there were strong indications that the Iraq authorities intended to contest the NFZ. SAM missile systems were deployed by the Iraqi force below the NFZ while a number of Iraqi Air Force aircraft began to make high-speed dashes int the NFZ. An Iraqi MiG-25 Foxbat was shot down by a USAF F-16 and Coalition forces began t prepare airstrikes to neutralize the threat to its aircraft operation in the NFZ.

The first package was launched on 13 January 1993 with around 100 aircraft participating The RAF contribution, codenamed Operation Ingleton, comprised four Tornado aircraft. AA support was provided by the Bahrain-based Victor K.2 of No. 55 Squadron.

Operation Allied Force

The bombing of Yugoslavia was NATO's military operation against the Serbian people durin the Kosovo War. According to NATO, the operation sought to stop human rights abuses i Kosovo and it was the first time that NATO used military force without the approval of the U Security Council. The air strikes lasted from 24 March to 10 June 1999. The bombings led to th eventual withdrawal of Yugoslav forces from Kosovo and the establishment of the UN Missio in Kosovo (UNMIK).

During the 1999 NATO bombing of Yugoslavia, VC10 tankers were stationed at Ancona AB i Southern Italy to refuel NATO aircraft in theatre. This allowed Tornado GR.1 fighter-bomber stationed at RAF Bruggen to conduct long-range strike missions against targets in Serbia. I addition, four Tristar aircraft were also deployed to Ancona in Italy, all in the tanking role.

Operation Veritas

Operation Veritas was the code name used for British military operations against the Taliban i Afghanistan during 2001. Primarily, the British forces played a supporting role to the US Operatio Enduring Freedom, although it was a significant contribution to the overall forces deployed.

VC10 aircraft from both Nos 10 and 101 Squadrons were based in Oman and were tasked i some of the very first missions, where they provided tanking capabilities to US carrier-base aircraft.

Operation Veritas also incorporated Operation Oracle (the UK component of coalitio operations against Al-Qaeda and Taliban forces within Afghanistan) and Operation Fingal (th UK contribution to the International Security Assistance Force established in January 2002), th latter of which was succeeded by Operation Herrick from 2002 onwards.

Four Tristar aircraft from No. 216 Squadron were deployed to Bahrain, where they provide air-to-air tanking facilities primarily for US Navy aircraft. No. 10 Squadron and No. 101 Squadro VC10 tanker aircraft remained on long-term deployment to the Middle East for twelve year ending just before the VC10 was withdrawn from service in 2013.

Operation Telic

Operation Telic was the code name given to the UK's military operations in Iraq during the US-led coalition, which was conducted between the start of the invasion on 19 March 2003 and the withdrawal of the last remaining British forces on 22 May 2011. Operation Telic was one of the largest deployments of British forces since the Second World War.

A VC10 wing was stationed at Prince Sultan AB in Saudi Arabia with a mixed fleet of seven VC10 aircraft from both Nos 10 and 101 Squadrons, where they supported Tornado GR.4, Harrier, Nimrod and Hercules operations. A single No. 216 Squadron Tristar aircraft was also deployed to the region.

In June 2009 the remaining VC10 aircraft, along with most of the remaining British military assets, were withdrawn from Iraq.

Operation Herrick

Operation Herrick was the name given to the British military operations in Afghanistan from 2002 until the end of combat operations in 2014. The British contribution was in support of the NATO-led International Security Assistance Force (ISAF), and in support of the US-led Operation Enduring Freedom.

By October 2014, the UK had ceased all combat operations in Afghanistan and withdrawn the last of its troops.

During the conflict, VC10 aircraft from both No. 10 and No. 101 Squadrons operated in support of RAF and other coalition forces, as did No. 216 Squadron Tristar aircraft.

Operation Ellamy

Operation Ellamy was the code name for the UK's participation in the military intervention in Libya in 2011. The operation was part of an international coalition aimed at enforcing a Libyan no-fly zone in accordance with United Nations Security Council Resolution (UNSCR) 1973, which stipulated that 'all necessary measures' should be taken to protect civilians.

During Operation Ellamy, a small number of VC10 aircraft were dispatched to bases in the Mediterranean and were used to refuel NATO strike aircraft being used in theatre. Initially, the RAF Tornado GR.4s were flown directly into theatre from their base at Marham with support from RAF VC10 tankers, but later these and a group of Typhoons were deployed to Gioia del Colle as No. 906 Expeditionary Air Wing (EAW). In addition, a No. 216 Squadron Tristar aircraft supported British air strikes on Libya on 19–20 March 2011 as part of the coalition operations.

Operation Shader

Operation Shader is the operational code name given to the UK's contributions in the ongoing military intervention against the Islamic State of Iraq and the Levant (ISIL). The operation began in Iraq on 26 September 2014, following a formal request from the Iraqi Government.

Initially, the operation began as a humanitarian relief effort but has since increased into Syria with surveillance flights. On 2 December 2015, the House of Commons approved British airstrikes against ISIL in Syria. The UK is one of several countries involved in the ongoing Syrian conflict that began in March 2011.

RAF tanking operations have been limited to the Voyager KC.3, supporting RAF Tornado GR.4 and Typhoon FGR.4 aircraft in theatre, while also providing their tanker/transport capabilities in re-supply operations into RAF Akrotiri.

Operation Corporate

During Operation Corporate – the recovery of the Falklands Islands after Argentine forces invaded on 2 April 1982 – Victor to Victor air-to-air refuelling was commonplace, especially during the Black Buck missions. These raids involved a single Vulcan bomber attacking the runway as well as other Argentine assets at Port Stanley and in order to get the Vulcan into theatre, it involved up to twenty-two different refuelling contacts of Victor to Victor and Victor to Vulcan aircraft. Each raid involved extraordinary planning and execution of the tanker tasking! (*Crown Copyright/Air Historical Branch image Falk-57-6*)

The view over the shoulder of the Hercules C.1P co-pilot as the aircraft takes on fuel from a Victor K.2 while en route from Ascension Island to Port Stanley in June 1982. At the outbreak of the Falklands conflict, the RAF's fleet of Hercules C.1 aircraft did not possess an air-to-air refuelling capability but this was hastily remedied by Marshall's of Cambridge, enabling the re-supply of troops engaged in the conflict. (*Marshall's of Cambridge*)

Operation Granby
Buccaneer S.2 XV352/U *Tamdhu* of the Lossiemouth Buccaneer Wing photographed while refuelling from No. 55 Squadron Victor K.2 XL164 during the latter part of Operation Granby. (*BAE Systems Heritage Collection*)

VC10 K.2 ZA144/E of No. 101 Squadron photographed while refuelling a pair of No. 6 Squadron Jaguar GR.1s. (*Crown Copyright/Air Historical Branch*)

No. 216 Squadron Tristar K.1 ZD949 was one of two Tristar aircraft to receive an unusual 'desert camouflage' during Operation Granby, which earned them the nickname 'Pink Pigs'. (*Crown Copyright/ Air Historical Branch image AHB-Slide-101Sqn-998*)

During Operation Granby, tanker support was often provided by Victor K.2 aircraft. Here, a No. 55 Squadron Victor K.2, XL161, provides fuel to a Buccaneer S.2B, XX901/N, along with an unidentified Tornado GR.1 coded 'N' carrying 'Snoopy Airways' titles. (*Crown Copyright/Air Historical Branch image GW-40*)

No. 101 Squadron VC10 K.2 ZA140/A refuelling a No. 11 Squadron Tornado F.3, ZE962/DL, over the desert during Operation Granby. (*Crown Copyright/Air Historical Branch*)

Operation Warden
A No. 10 Squadron VC10 C.1K photographed while refuelling a US Navy EA-6B Prowler during Operation Warden on 27 August 2000. At the time, the No. 10 Squadron VC10 aircraft were deployed to Incirlik Air Base in Turkey. (*Crown Copyright/Air Historical Branch image VC10-04*)

Operation Veritas
A No. 101 Squadron VC10 refuels an unidentified US Navy F-18A from VF-97 on 15 December 2001 during Operation Veritas. (*Crown Copyright/Air Historical Branch image VC10 Tanking US F18*)

Three Tornado GR.1A aircraft from No. II (AC) Squadron refuel from a No. 101 Squadron VC10 during Operation Veritas. (*Crown Copyright/Air Historical Branch*)

Operation Telic

A No. 101 Squadron VC10 K.3 refuels a pair of Tornado F.3s during Operation Telic in April 2003. (*Crown Copyright/Air Historical Branch image MNT-003-0995/SAC Sarah Burrows*)

No. 216 Squadron Tristar K.1 ZD951 refuelling a coalition forces US Navy EA-6B Prowler of VAQ-141 during Operation Telic. (*Crown Copyright/Air Historical Branch image MNT-03-003-0224*)

A RAF Tornado F.3 takes on fuel from a USAF KC-135 before continuing its patrol over the Gulf during Operation Telic. The tanker is from the 117 Air Refuelling Wing (ARW), Air Mobility Command (AMC), and was using a special hose and drogue extension which has been added to its flying boom to enable it to refuel the Tornado. (*Crown Copyright/Air Historical Branch image MNT-008-495-unc/Cpl Jez Doak*)

Operation Herrick

A US Navy F/A-18C coded 'NK-306' from VF-113 holds his position on Tristar K.1 ZD951 as 'NK-402' takes on fuel from the tanker over Southern Afghanistan on 9 October 2008. Both F/A-18C aircraft were assigned to CVW-14 embarked aboard the Nimitz-class aircraft carrier USS *Ronald Reagan* (CVN 76). The carrier strike group, which was deployed to the US 5th Fleet area of responsibility, was providing support to coalition forces on the ground in Afghanistan. (*US Department of Defence photo by Cmdr. Erik Etz, U.S. Navy*)

VC10 C.1K XV102/T was photographed while refuelling a pair of No. 1 Squadron Harrier GR.9 aircraft during their deployment to Afghanistan under Operation Herrick between April and June 2009. (*Crown Copyright/Air Historical Branch image F540-0609-WIT-1 SQN-040*)

Operation Ellamy
VC10 C.1K XV106/W sits on the runway at Brize Norton on 19 March 2011 just ahead of its departure. XV106 was one of a number of VC10 tankers that accompanied Tornado GR.4 aircraft from RAF Marham that struck Libyan air defences in what was the longest strike mission flown by the RAF since the Black Buck operations during the Falklands conflict. (*Crown Copyright/Air Historical Branch image 45152514/SAC Neil Chapman*)

No. 101 Squadron VC10 aircraft were supporting a number of different air arms participating in Operation Ellamy, including the Canadian Armed Forces (CAF). In this image, taken on 7 July 2011, a CAF CF-18A, serial number 188746, was refuelling from the VC10's starboard wing pod. (*Crown Copyright/Air Historical Branch image Ellamy-906-110707-0275-0208/SAC Sally Raimondo*)

Operation Shader
Tornado GR.4 ZA609/072 photographed while receiving fuel from a Voyager KC.2 during Operation Shader on 22 October 2015. At the time of the image, No. 9 Squadron from RAF Marham were operating the Tornado Detachment (TORDET) out of RAF Akrotiri. (*Crown Copyright/Air Historical Branch image AUAB-20151022-138-240/Cpl Alex Scott*)

AAR Equipment and Applications

No. 101 Squadron VC10 K.2 ZA141/B refuels a pair of No. 31 Squadron Tornado GR.1 aircraft (ZG794/DJ and ZD790/DL) in a North Sea tow-line using the FRL Mk 32/2800 hose-drum units (HDUs) mounted on the underside of each wing. A further FRL Mk 17B HDU was installed in a specially constructed bay in the underside of the rear fuselage. (*Keith Wilson*)

The earliest air-to-air refuelling equipment dates back to the barnstorming days of the 1920s and '30s when attempts were made to remain aloft for the longest possible time. It was often done as more of a stunt than a serious attempt to extend the range or increase the payload of an aircraft of the day.

Initial trials with AAR had been conducted in April 1923 using a pair of US Army Air Service DH.4B aircraft – one as receiver and the other as the tanker. The tanker dangled a 50-foot length of refuelling hose terminating in a trigger nozzle, which was grabbed by the observer in the receiver aircraft before being inserted into the open filler neck of the receiver's fuel tank. Controlled by the observer, the fuel was fed by gravity. Using this rudimentary methodology, it permitted a record of 37 hours and 15 minutes to be achieved over the period of 23/24 April. The event was well-publicised across the world and the success of the AAR encouraged others on both sides of the Atlantic to attempt similar experiments, including the Royal Aircraft Establishment (RAE) at Farnborough as well as by Captain Pierre Weiss and Adj Van Caudenburg in France. However, while a number of further records were set and broken, the rudimentary nature of the equipment prevented those involved in taking the skill much farther forward other than purely for record-breaking purposes.

In 1932, Sir Alan Cobham started to take a serious interest in the AAR process and in 1934 formed Flight Refuelling Limited. During the same year, he had unsuccessfully attempted to fly non-stop from Portsmouth to Karachi utilising AAR, employing Handley Page W.10 tankers refuelling Cobham's own Airspeed Courier G-ABXN. Interestingly, the refuelling hose wa caught by a member of the Courier crew using a walking stick!

Cross-Over Contact

Meanwhile, Squadron Leader R. L. R. Atcherley had started experiments in AAR with the RA at Farnborough using what was being called the 'Cross-Over Contact' method. This involved th trailing – from the receiver – of a horizontal line, terminating in a grapnel, while the tanker trailed weighted line. Then, by flying from side to side above and astern of it, the tanker enabled a contac to be made between the two lines. Once this was achieved, the refuelling hose could be passed from tanker to receiver by hauling in the receiver's line. A draft of the method was submitted to the Ai Ministry but, at the time, was not considered to be an improvement over existing methods.

Looped-Hose Method

After Flight Refuelling Limited (FRL) moved to Ford aerodrome in Sussex, they took over th work of Squadron Leader Atcherley at the RAE Farnborough. It proved to be a progressivel successful partnership, and the implementation of Cobham's and Atcherley's ideas becam known as the looped-hose method. In this method, the receiver trailed a hauling line terminatin in a 55 lb sinker weight and pawl, while the tanker flew to the side of, and below the receiver (se diagram on page 102). The tanker than fired a line with a contractor hook, which – hopefully crossed over the receiver's hauling line and engaged the pawl grapnel. The tanker then haule in the receiver's hauling line and climbed above the receiver, remaining astern so that when th contractor hook was fully hauled in, the hook and sinker weight were removed from the haulin line and the refuelling hose connected to it. Once all of this had been successfully achieved, th receiver hauled the refuelling hose until the nozzle engaged the receiver's coupling. The tanke and receiver were then required to fly in careful formation while the fuel was transferred.

On completion, the receiver would once again trail the released hauling line and refuellin hose. After a certain length had been trailed the tanker would then climb and turn away from the receiver, causing a weak link in the hauling line to break.

Despite its unquestionable capabilities, the looped-hose method was a complex engineerin solution that required a high standard of flying skill from all participants!

Probe and Drogue Arrives

Although, in March 1949, a modified version of the looped-hose method had successfully enable four Boeing KB-29M tanker aircraft to refuel a Boeing B-50A, *Lucky Lady II*, for it to complet a 94-hour, non-stop around-the-world flight, the system clearly needed further developmen to refuel single-seat fighter aircraft. FRL's response was the probe and drogue system, whic was demonstrated to a delegation of USAF officers just six months after the requirement wa mooted. On 7 August 1949, an FRL Lancaster tanker and Meteor receiver aircraft enabled a worl record for jet aircraft endurance of 12 hours and 3 minutes to be achieved. The success of th new and innovative design was obvious and was to have a massive impact on FRL's fortunes.

This method of military air-to-air refuelling was soon adopted by the RAF, USAF, US Navy (USN and US Marine Corps (USMC), although later the USAF would pursue the Flying Boom methoc The Korean conflict saw the first use of hose and drogue refuelling in theatre. Carrier-launche twin-engine North American AJ-2 Savage tankers fitted with a single US-manufactured hos drum unit designed by FR Inc. undertook demanding refuelling tasks, including the refuellin of Grumman Panther aircraft using a HDU mounted in the fuselage with the drogue extende ut through what had been the jet's former exhaust outlet from the third – turbojet engine – which had been removed. US Navy AD-6 Skyraiders were also equipped as AAR tankers while the USAF employed probe-and-drogue-equipped Boeing KB-29 tankers to refuel both F-80A and F-84 jet fighters directly into the probe normally mounted in their wing tip pods.

Later, the Soviet Union reverse-engineered the NATO hose and drogue system – called the UPAZ (Unified Refuelling Pod) – so all Russian aircraft are equipped with probe and drogue equipment.

Buddy-Buddy tanking

Using the hose and drogue method, the USN and USMC later perfected the Buddy-Buddy system of refuelling support, permitting a fighter or strike aircraft equipped with a simple refuelling unit (HDU), usually in conjunction with additional fuel tank space, to supply other similar types and extend both their range and payload.

Buddy-Buddy tanking would later become an important aspect of both Royal Navy and RAF operations in the future, with the system being employed to good effect on RN aircraft carrier operations with Scimitar, Sea Vixen and Buccaneer aircraft all providing an extra and often important aspect of operations at sea.

The technique was also employed to great effect by the RAF with their fleet of Buccaneer aircraft. It was considered by the RAF for Tornado GR.1 operations when, in August 1993, a plan was considered to re-use the Mk 20B HDUs from eight Victor K.2s of No. 55 Squadron that were being withdrawn from use on 1 October 1993. The plan was to add a modified Mk 20G refuelling pod to the underside of the fuselage and then spread the Buddy-Buddy capable Tornado fleet throughout all of the service's GR.1 squadrons. Although the design work was undertaken by FRL and tested at Boscombe Down, the capability was never ordered. Later, however, the Italian Air Force did order the buddy system for its Tornado IDS fleet, as did the German Navy. Both organisations selected the Sargent Fletcher 28-300 refuelling store for the role.

Interestingly, another air arm to use to the Buddy-Buddy system to good effect is that of the Soviet Union and, later, Russia, who have equipped some of their Su-24MK Fencer and Su-31 aircraft for the role.

The Flying Boom

One of the major limitations of the hose-and-drogue refuelling system is the rate of fuel flow physically possible through the hoses. Most FRL pods are capable of placing around 3,000 ppm (pounds of fuel per minute) into a receiver aircraft. This is more than adequate for most fighter aircraft but when refuelling very large aircraft – in particular the B-58 and B-52 – a much higher fuel flow was required.

Consequently, in the late 1940s, General Curtis LeMay, Commander of the Strategic Air Command (SAC), asked Boeing to develop a refuelling system that could transfer at a much higher flow rate. This resulted in the Boeing Flying Boom system, a rigid, telescoping tube of up to 60 feet in length. Their physical size meant they could only be fitted to large aircraft and the initial choice was a modified Boeing B-29, which was fitted with the first boom in 1950. Later, 16 B-29s were converted at the Renton, Washington, plant to B-29Ps with the addition of a flying boom. Later, a number of KB-50D aircraft were also fitted with the flying boom. Next to receive the flying boom modification was the Boeing KC-97. However, while all of these piston-powered tanker aircraft were comfortable refuelling at similar speeds to their piston-powered bombers, all lacked the speed and performance required to refuel jet fighter aircraft at altitude, with many receivers flying at close to their minimum manoeuvring speed during the refuelling process.

Boeing B-52 bombers usually needed to lower flaps and the rear undercarriage in order to refuel from a C-97, and often in a gentle dive.

One solution was to add a pair of General Electric J-47 jet engines in under-wing pods to produce the KC-97L. It increased the performance of the tanker but the aircraft now needed to carry two types of fuel for their operation – Avgas for the four piston-engines and Avtur for the J47 jet engines. This requirement reduced the overall capability and effectiveness of the KC-97L as a tanker aircraft.

However, Boeing were aware of the limitations of the piston-powered tanker and were involved in a major design study with their prototype four-engine jet transport – the Model 367-80 – which was built with both commercial and military tanker operations in mind. The potential of the military tanker version was soon seen and shortly after the prototype made its first flight on 15 July 1954, Boeing received an initial order for twenty-nine KC-135A aircraft. The prototype – serial number 55-3118 – made its first flight on 31 August 1956. Eventually, a total of 820 C-135 aircraft were manufactured.

The USAF continued the Flying Boom philosophy with their KC-10 Extender tanker transport which entered service in March 1981. Meanwhile, the latest generation KC-46 Pegasus tanker transport is a military development of the successful Boeing 767 commercial airliner and, once again, features the Flying Boom. The first KC-46 aircraft was delivered to McConnell AFB, Kansas, on 25 January 2019.

RAF Continues with the Probe and Drogue

While the USAF was developing the Flying Boom tanker principles, the RAF continued down the probe and drogue route. After trials with the Lancaster and Lincoln aircraft had come to an end, a modified Canberra B.2 (WH734) effectively became the RAF's first jet tanker. Trials were conducted at Boscombe Down in July 1953 using a FRL Mk XV HDU and later a Mk 20A pod but the project was not developed into orders.

That honour was saved for the Vickers Valiant when B.1 WZ376 was modified as a tanker and WZ390 as the receiver for trials at Boscombe Down in November 1955. A Mk XVI HDU was installed into the bomb bay of the Valiant tanker (now designated B(K).1) and while initial trials showed some problems with a bow wave around the drogue, these were later cured with a modified ventilated, solid drogue.

Eventually a total of fifty-eight Valiant B(K).1 and B(PR)K.1 aircraft were modified into tanker/receivers where the tanker aircraft operated with Nos 214 and 90 Squadrons. The Valiant remained in service until the complete fleet was withdrawn from use on 26 January 1965 and scrapped following the discovery of metal fatigue in the main spars in December 1964.

After the Valiant was withdrawn, the Victor K.1 tanker entered service as its replacement – initially as a two-point tanker but later as a three-point tanker. The initial refuelling equipment was a pair of wing-mounted FRL Mk 20B HDUs that had been developed for use on the Royal Navy Scimitar and Sea Vixen Buddy-Buddy tanking solutions, and were supplemented by a single fuselage-mounted Mk 17. The first four conversions were delivered to No. 55 Squadron in May and June 1965.

Later, an order was placed for the conversion of twenty-nine Victor B.2 and SR.2 aircraft into three-point K.2 tankers, although this order was reduced to twenty-four owing to a Treasury economy campaign in April 1975.

Refurbished Mk 17B HDUs Provide an Interim Solution

In 1982, as an interim measure following the consumption of a large part of the Victor K.2s fatigue life during the Falklands conflict, six Vulcan aircraft were converted into single-point anker aircraft using refurbished Mk 17B HDUs and the aircraft were now designated Vulcan K.2. All were delivered to No. 50 Squadron at RAF Waddington, where they operated in support of the defence of UK airspace until being retired in March 1984 when No. 50 Squadron was disbanded.

Around the same time, six Hercules C.1 aircraft were also modified to single-point tankers. Once again, FRL Mk 17B HDUs were installed into the aircraft, the conversions being carried out by Marshall's of Cambridge. The HDU was installed onto the rear cargo ramp and the drogue towage tunnel, together with the contact lights, would be located into the upper cargo door. These single-point tankers were mainly used in support of the Falkland Islands, in particular refuelling the RAF's fleet of Hercules C.1P transport aircraft replenishing supplies into theatre.

Converted Airliners

With the Victor K.2 rapidly reaching the end of its fatigue life, it was important for the RAF to acquire a new strategic tanking capability. The VC10 was chosen and a number of former civilian airline aircraft were acquired for conversion, consisting of five standard VC10s (series 1101) from Gulf Air and four Super VC10s (series 1154) from East African Airways. Later, a further fourteen Super VC10 aircraft were acquired from British Airways and placed into storage. All conversion work was undertaken by British Aerospace at Filton. The first VC10 K.2 conversion (ZA141) flew at Filton on 22 June 1982 and, following clearance trials with Boscombe Down, the type began to enter service with No. 101 Squadron at Brize Norton in May 1984.

Primarily intended to refuel air defence fighters including the Tornado and Phantom, the VC10 tankers were each fitted with a pair of the new under-wing-mounted FRL Mk 32/2800 HDUs, along with a single Mk 17B HDU located in the rear fuselage. An additional five cylindrical fuel tanks were added to the fuselages of the K.2 and K.3 variants, thereby significantly increasing their strategic capability, and the VC10 was a particular popular tanker aircraft with its receiver crews and served well in a number of theatres.

Tristar

In 1982, a decision was taken to purchase six British Airways Tristar 500 aircraft and a contract was awarded to Marshall's of Cambridge to commence a military tanker/transport conversion programme, although Flight Refuelling had a major part to play in the design and manufacture of the AAR equipment. The programme was later increased to nine aircraft when three former Pan Am Tristar aircraft were acquired, all to be operated by No. 216 Squadron at RAF Brize Norton.

In order to fulfil their proposed roles, large cargo doors were fitted to the forward fuselage of all of the aircraft, while six of them were also fitted with twin Mk 17T HDUs in the rear fuselage along with underfloor fuel tanks in the forward cargo compartment. The twin HDUs were located within a pressure box, with access to them being through a large access door on the starboard side of the box structure. An in-flight refuelling probe was also fitted to all nine aircraft.

A proposal was also considered to fit a pair of Mk 32A refuelling pods on under-wing stations, to permit the Tristar to become a three-point tanker, but issues with hose length and the close proximity to other refuelling aircraft prevented it reaching fruition.

VC10 C.1K

In 1991, Flight Refuelling commenced converting the RAF's fleet of VC10 C.1 transport aircraft into two-point tankers. Once again, the equipment of choice was a pair of FRL Mk 32 HDUs, one being located under each wing. However, the Mk 32 refuelling pod incorporated the introduction of a fault-finding system capable of informing the operator of any malfunction within the pod.

All thirteen VC10 C.1s then in service with No. 10 Squadron at Brize Norton were converted to C.1K standards and had re-entered service as two-point tankers by 1996.

A330MRTT Voyager

In January 2004, it was announced that the A330MRTT had been selected to provide tanking service for the RAF for the next thirty years under the Future Strategic Tanker Aircraft (FSTA) programme, replacing the VC10 and Tristar aircraft remaining in service. Later, in 2008, the UK Ministry of Defence signed a lease agreement with AirTanker to provide fourteen aircraft with the first planned to enter service in 2011. Two versions – the Voyager KC.2 and KC.3 – were ordered, and by March 2016 all had been delivered to the RAF.

The Voyager KC.2 version is a two-point tanker, fitted with a pair of Cobham (formerly FRL) 905E under-wing refuelling pods while the Voyager KC.3 has, in addition to the wing pods, a Cobham 805E fuselage refuelling unit (FRU). Interestingly, the A330MRTT is capable of carrying an Aerial Refuelling Boom System (ARBS); although the RAF initially declined this option, it is still available.

HDUs

Both the 905E (wing) and 805E (fuselage) pods fitted to the Voyager represent the most advanced air refuelling system in production today. Fuels flow rates are a staggering 450 US gpm (US gallons per minute) for the 905E and 700 US gpm for the fuselage-mounted 805E. That said, Cobham offer a variety of refuelling pods to suit a diverse range of air-to-air refuelling assets in service throughout the world – including packages for the A400M, KC-46, KC-390, KC-10, KC-135 and even the MV-22 Osprey. Some of these are illustrated in the images that follow.

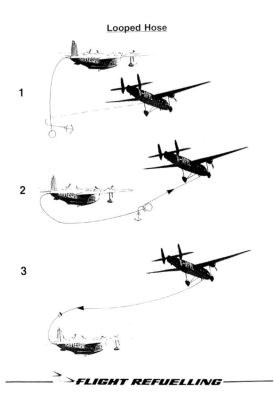

A Flight Refuelling Limited diagram demonstrating the early looped hose method of air-to-air refuelling. (*Cobham plc*)

A view of the fuselage-mounted FRL Mk 16 HDU fitted to the Valiant tanker, as seen from the cockpit of a Victor B.1 receiver. While initial trials showed some problems with a bow wave around the original drogue fitted to the test aircraft, these were later cured with the fitting of a modified ventilated, solid drogue, as shown here. (*Cohham plc*)

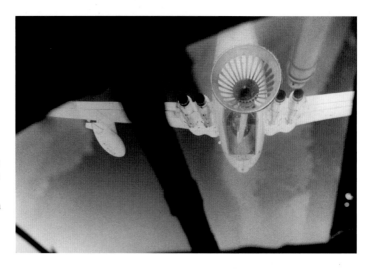

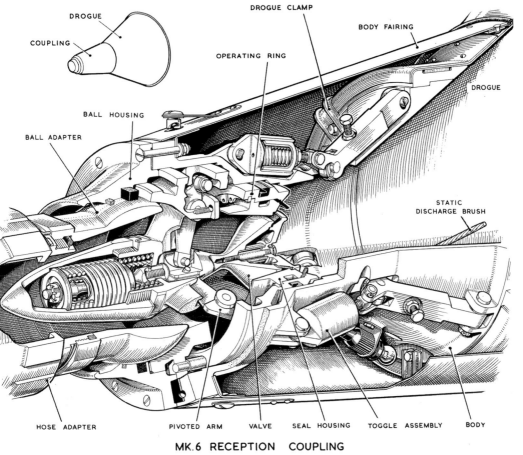

MK.6 RECEPTION COUPLING

A schematic diagram of the Mk 6 reception coupling as fitted to Valiant trials aircraft WZ376 and '390. Following extensive refuelling trials a number of modifications were completed and the Mk 9 drogue was fitted to all Valiant B(K).1 and B(PR)K.1 receiver aircraft, used in conjunction with the FRL Mk 16 Hose Drum Unit (HDU) (see overleaf). (*Brooklands Museum*)

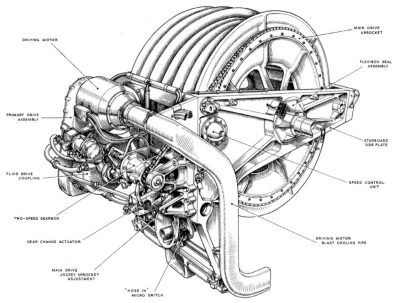

DRIVING MOTOR

PRIMARY DRIVE
ASSEMBLY

FLUID DRIVE
COUPLING

TWO-SPEED GEARBOX

GEAR CHANGE ACTUATOR

MAIN DRIVE
JOCKEY SPROCKET
ADJUSTMENT

"HOSE IN"
MICRO SWITCH

MAIN DRIVE
SPROCKET

FLEXIBOX SEAL
ASSEMBLY

STARBOARD
SIDE PLATE

SPEED CONTROL
UNIT

DRIVING MOTOR
BLAST COOLING PIPE

MK.16 HOSE DRUM UNIT, STARBOARD SIDE

A schematic diagram of the FRL Mk 16 Hose Drum Unit (HDU) as fitted to the Valiant B(K).1 and B/K(PR).1 tanker aircraft, and used in conjunction with the FRL Mk 6 probe (see previous page). (*Brooklands Museum*)

While the RAF pursued the concept of hose and drogue refuelling, the USAF decided to go down the flying boom solution originally devised by Boeing. Initially, the slow speed of early piston-powered tankers had made AAR difficult for the smaller fast jet receivers, although this changed with the arrival of the Boeing KC-135A. 62-3572 is shown here refuelling four Republic F-105 Thunderchief aircraft ahead of a Linebacker operation during the Vietnam War. (*Crown Copyright/Air Historical Branch image reference Humphrey Linebacker-17*)

The receiver's view as a No. 12 Squadron Buccaneer S.2 approaches the basket on a No. 57 Squadron Victor K.1A, XH618, in June 1970. Originally configured as a two-point tanker, the K.1 variant was initially fitted with a pair of under-wing-mounted FRL Mk 20B HDUs. Later, many of the K.1 aircraft received an additional rear fuselage-mounted FRL Mk 17B HDU, converting them to three-point tankers. (*Crown Copyright/Air Historical Branch image reference TN-1-6232-37*)

A Victor K.2, XL233, of No. 232 OCU refuels a Coningsby-based Phantom FGR.2 of No. 29 Squadron high over the North Sea in January 1975. Twenty-four surplus Victor B.2 aircraft were converted into K.2 three-point tanker variants from 1972 to 1975. Each had its wing span reduced to 113 feet to extend its fatigue life and was fitted with a pair of under-wing-mounted FRL Mk 20B HDUs along with a single FRL Mk 17 HDU mounted at the rear of the fuselage. (*Crown Copyright/Air Historical Branch image reference TN-1-7136-18*)

Technicians inspecting the centreline hose and drogue fitted to No. 57 Squadron Victor K.1A XH620 at RAF Marham in January 1973. (*Crown Copyright/ Air Historical Branch image reference TN-1-6704-31*)

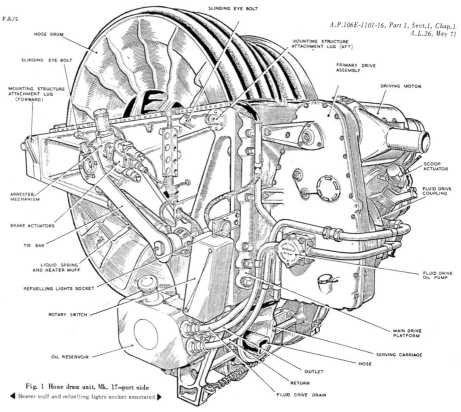

A schematic diagram of the FRL Mk 17 Hose Drum Unit (HDU) as fitted into the rear fuselage of the Victor K.1 and K.2 three-point tanker aircraft. (*Brooklands Museum*)

Following the consumption of a large part of the Victor K.2s' fatigue life during the Falklands conflict, six Vulcan aircraft (including XM571 seen here) were converted into single-point tanker aircraft using refurbished Mk 17B HDUs and the aircraft were now designated Vulcan K.2. All were delivered to No. 50 Squadron, where they operated in support of the defence of UK airspace until retired in 1984. (*Cobham plc*)

The refurbished Mk 17B HDUs fitted to the rear fuselage of the Vulcan K.2 of No. 50 Squadron can be seen during routine maintenance to one of the aircraft at RAF Waddington in August 1983. (*Crown Copyright/ Air Historical Branch TN-1-9508-19*)

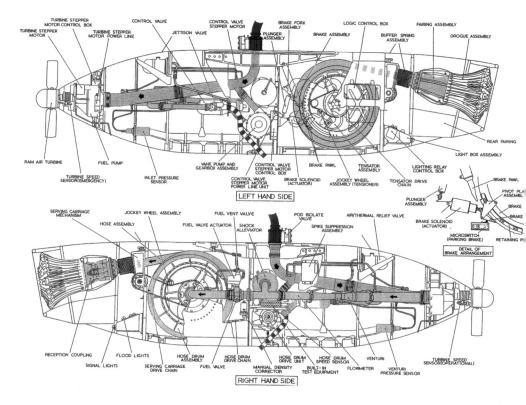

Schematic diagram of the FRL Mk 32-2800 refuelling pod, as fitted to the VC10 K.2 and K.3 aircraft. (*via Andy Townsend*)

During the conversion programme undertaken by British Aerospace, the former airline VC10 aircraft were converted into K.2 and K.3 tanker aircraft, which included the fitting of a pair of new under-wing-mounted FRL Mk 32-2800 refuelling pod (shown here), along with a single Mk 17B HDU located in the rear fuselage. (*BAE Systems Heritage image A7052D*)

In addition to the fitting of three HDUs on each VC.10 K.2 and K.3 conversion, additional fuel tanks were installed into the fuselage of each aircraft. The K.2 had capacity for an additional 17,925 gallons (around 64 tons) while the K.3 had provision for an increased capacity of 19,365 gallons (around 69 tons); the extra fuel on the K.3 was made possible by the addition of a fuel tank located in the aircraft's fin. (*BAE Systems image A6480 via Bristol Aero Collection Trust*)

In 1989, approval was granted for the remaining thirteen VC10 C.1 aircraft of No. 10 Squadron to be converted by Flight Refuelling Limited at Hurn into two-point C.1K tankers, with the addition of a pair of FRL Mk 32 HDUs; with one being located under each wing. Here, XV101 was photographed over the North Sea refuelling a pair of No. 29 Squadron Tornado F.3s – ZG733/BK and the uncoded ZE834 – from RAF Coningsby. (*Keith Wilson*)

The receiver's view during buddy-buddy tanking operations in a No. 12 Squadron Buccaneer S.2, XX885, call sign 'Jackal 2', during operations at 18,000 feet to the north-east of Scotland on 3 December 1992. Another No. 12 Squadron Buccaneer S.2B (XW530 'K2P18') is providing the fuel. (*Keith Wilson*)

In August 1993, the RAF reviewed a plan to re-use the Mk 20B HDUs from eight Victor K.2 aircraft of No. 55 Squadron that were surplus to requirements as the aircraft were being withdrawn from use on 1 October 1993. The plan was to add a reworked Mk 20G refuelling pod to the underside of the Tornado GR.1 fuselage and then spread the proposed buddy-buddy tanking capable Tornado fleet of aircraft throughout the service's GR.1 squadrons. Although the design work was undertaken by FRL and tested at the A&AEE, Boscombe Down, the capability was never ordered. The buddy-buddy tanking capability would have been a major attribute to the RAF's GR.1 force! (*Cobham plc*)

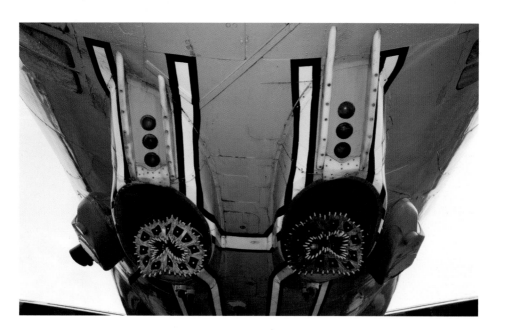

Six former British Airways Tristar 500 aircraft were converted by Marshall's of Cambridge into single-point tanks with the fitting of a pair of FRL Mk 17T HDUs. Two HDUs were fitted to the rear fuselage of each aircraft to provide redundancy in the unfortunate event of a HDU failure. The Mk 17T HDU was a derivative of the earlier Mk 17B but had the hose length reduced from 80 feet to just 70 feet. All of the converted Tristar aircraft were operated by No. 216 Squadron at Brize Norton until retired from service in March 2014. Tristar K.1 ZD948 was photographed while in storage at Bruntingthorpe on 17 July 2018. (*Keith Wilson*)

In addition to the pair of Mk 17T HDUs fitted to the rear fuselage, the conversion programme also included the fitting of an air-to-air refuelling control console, fitted into the cockpit at the flight engineer's station. A CCTV system was also added, providing the crew of the tanker aircraft with a view of AAR proceedings, as seen fitted here on Tristar KC.1 ZD953. (*Keith Wilson*)

One of the limitations of a tanker fitted with just the flying boom system was its inability to refuel aircraft requiring a hose and drogue system. However, the final twenty KC-10 aircraft featured a mixed refuelling system of hose and drogue and flying boom, allowing it to refuel the aircraft of the US Air Force, US Navy, US Marine Corps as well as those of other allied forces – something which proved particularly beneficial during Operation Desert Shield, Desert Storm, Enduring Freedom and Iraqi Freedom, in addition to operations in Kosovo. (*Cobham plc reference 10852B*)

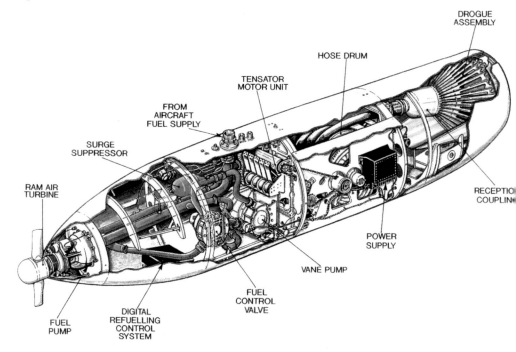

By 1988, the Cobham 750 series refuelling pods were being fitted to the under-wing stations of the USAF KC-10 aircraft, along with an FR600 Fuselage Refuelling Unit. (*Cobham plc*)

The fifth KC-130F Hercules tanker built seen during refuelling operations with a pair of Marine Corps CH-53 Sea Stallion helicopters, each carrying a sling-loaded LAV-25 armoured vehicle. This KC-130F (Bureau Number 148248/BH-248) entered service in 1961 and was later assigned to VMGR-252 at MCAS Cherry Point, North Carolina. The aircraft was retired from service in October 2004 and is currently held in the 309 AMARG. (*Lockheed via Cobham plc*)

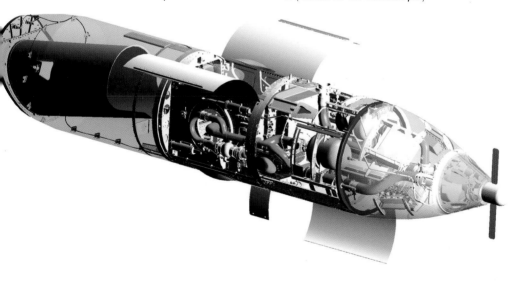

The fifth-generation Cobham 905E pod as fitted to the under-wing stations of the A330 MRTT and operated by the RAF. The 905E pod can deliver fuel at up to 450 US gallons per minute at a delivery pressure of up to 50 psi using a hose length of up to 90 feet, all within an operating speed range of 185 to 350 knots. (*Cobham plc*)

The Future of AAR

On 22 April 2015, the US Navy's unmanned Northrop-Grumman X-47B UCAV (Unmanned Combat A
Vehicle) received fuel from an Omega Aerial Refuelling Services K-707 tanker, N707MQ, while operatin
in the Atlantic Test Ranges over the Chesapeake Bay. This test marked the first time an unmanned aircra
was refuelled in flight. (*US Navy/Liz Wolter via Omega*)

Air-to-air refuelling has come a very long way since the earliest trials back in 1923, using a 50-foc
length of hose dangled into the slipstream by a 'tanker' which required the observer in th
'receiver' aircraft to catch and then manoeuvre the trigger nozzle into the open filler neck of th
fuel tank. While the earliest AAR developments and trials were usually around attempts to brea
records, it was the advent of the Cold War and military air-to-air refuelling requirements tha
have driven AAR developments – very rapidly – ever since. The pace of change within AAR doe
not look like slowing down; in fact the developments seem to be going at a faster pace than eve

RAF AAR Developments

Following the signing of the lease agreement on 27 March 2008 with Air Tanker, to be funde
under a Private Finance Initiative, the RAF's primary air-to-air tanking force now consists of
fleet of fourteen Voyager aircraft – well almost!

It has a 'core fleet' of ten aircraft, while the remaining four aircraft are available to the RAF,
and when required. According to the agreement, these are retained by AirTanker who are free
offer them on the civilian charter market, less their specialist AAR equipment.

Three of the aircraft are two-point tankers (KC.2) while seven are equipped as three-poir
tankers (KC.3), all utilising Cobham hose-and-drogue systems. What they do lack is the means t
refuel some RAF assets such as the E-3D Sentry, Rivet Joint and the A330 MRTT aircraft itse

Perhaps, in the future, the RAF may acquire one or more A330 MRTT tanker aircraft equipped with the Aerial Refuelling Boom System (ARBS), which in addition to being able to refuel the RAF aircraft above would also make the aircraft suitable for the refuelling of a wide variety of NATO fast jet aircraft including the F-16 – providing a significant improvement in allied flexibility.

Airbus A400M Atlas

Airbus Defence and Space have been working on a tanker version of their A400M Atlas transport aircraft. So far, it has been offered with Cobham refuelling equipment: a pair of under-wing-mounted 908E Wing Dispense Equipment (WDE) units, each providing a fuel flow rate of up 400 US gallons per minute, in the two-point tanker role. By adding a single 808E Hose Drum Unit (HDU) fitted in the rear of the fuselage section, providing a fuel flow rate of up to 600 US gallons per minute, it offers a very respectable performance in the three-point role. Interestingly, all of the AAR equipment can be added or removed in a 'quick role change'. Airbus claims that the aircraft, if fitted with hard points, fuel lines and electrical connections in the wings, can be re-configured into a two-point tanker in less than two hours.

The A400M carries up to 50.5 tonnes (111,330 lb) of fuel in its wing and centre wing box. Two additional cargo tanks can also be installed, providing an additional 5.7 tonnes (12,600 lbs) of fuel each. Interestingly, the fuel carried in the extra tanks can be of a different nature to the fuel in the main tanks, enabling the A400M to cater for the differing requirements of receivers. Furthermore, because of the low fuel consumption of the A400M, it has the potential 'fuel-give-away' of 34 tonnes on a typical tanking mission, where it would loiter for up to 2 hours at a range of 500 n.m. from its base.

It has already been trialled with a variety of fast jet receivers on the wing hoses, as well as the C-295, C-130 and even another A400M on the centreline hose, making it quite a large buddy-buddy tanker! As a receiver, the A400M is equipped with a probe mounted above the cockpit, which can easily be removed when not required.

However, while trials undertaken in its current tanker configuration with helicopters have proven to be possible when flown by test pilots, it would not satisfy the more demanding safety margin in emergency conditions required for operational pilots. Consequently, development of this is being delayed until later in the programme.

In addition to an order for twenty-two aircraft for the RAF (of which twenty have been delivered at the time of writing), the A400M has been ordered by the air forces of France, Germany, Malaya, Spain and Turkey. So far, AAR testing has been conducted with aircraft in the colours of Spain and Germany. Perhaps, if the RAF were to have four or more of their aircraft configured in a quick-change AAR role, it would provide the RAF with a capable and versatile tactical tanking option?

USAF Developments

After having 'won' the bidding process against Airbus to supply the next generation of tanker aircraft for the USAF, Boeing have employed no less than six different airframes to achieve both a civilian Type Certificate with the Federal Aviation Authority (FAA) and a Military Type Certificate (MTC). In September 2018, they achieved the former with the granting of an STC (Supplemental Type Certificate) from the FAA and hope to complete the MTC by July 2019. This landmark will allow the new KC-46A Pegasus to join the USAF, initially replacing some of the older KC-135 aircraft in service.

The six aircraft involved in the programme completed 3,500 flight hours and offloaded more than 3 million pounds of fuel during refuelling flights with an assortment of receivers, including F-18, F/A-18, AV-8B, C-17, A-10, KC-10, KC-135 and KC-46 aircraft.

The KC-46A is somewhat unique in the tanking world as it is fitted with a flying boom as well as two Cobham RP-910E-75 Wing Air Refuelling Pods (WARP) and a Cobham FR-600-84MDF Centreline Drogue System (CDS). The flying boom permits the transfer of fuel at a rate of up to 1,200 US gallons per minute while each of the three hose-and-drogue units on the aircraft will transfer fuel at up to 400 US gallons per minute. Once in service, and although both smaller and with less payload than the A330MRTT, this flexibility will allow the KC-46A to refuel allied and coalition military aircraft in addition to the USAF, US Navy and US Marine Corps assets.

The KC-46A is derived from Boeing's commercial 767 airframe and, so far, Boeing has received orders for the first thirty-four of an expected order for seventy-nine tankers for the US Air Force. It is almost certain that over a period of time, this number will be increased to eventually replace the entire fleet of long-serving KC-135 tankers still in service.

US Navy Developments

The US Navy and Marine Corps have continued to place their faith in the venerable Hercules aircraft as its current tanker of choice. The US Marine Corps have received almost fifty of the seventy-nine KC-130J tankers on order, replacing older KC-130F, KC-130R and KC-130T variants although one USMC reserve unit will retain twelve KC-130T aircraft. Meanwhile the US Navy continues to operate a large fleet of KC-130T aircraft.

But what comes after the Hercules? At present, both services are looking at providing their larger helicopters with an air-to-air refuelling capability. Cobham have been working closely with both in an effort to find solutions to helicopter receivers as well as tankers. New probes have been designed, allowing a range of USN and USMC helicopters to rapidly convert into air refuelling receivers. The capability effectively removes the need for an auxiliary fuel tank for extended operations, which in turn permits the maximum possible payload to be carried throughout the mission. Some probes are of a fixed length while others can be telescopically extended beyond the main rotor disc to provide a safe separation during refuelling.

In addition, Cobham has designed the Cobham V-22 Aerial Refuelling System (VARS) consisting of a FR-300 hose drum unit to operate from within the MV-22B Osprey tanker, and trials with a variety of receivers, including F/A-18 aircraft, are progressing well.

In addition, the US Navy has been exploring the potential of unmanned aerial vehicles (UAVs) in the tanker role (see below).

Advent of Third-Party Independent Tanker Operators

One of the major changes to have affected the military tanker market in the last ten years is the advent of third party independent tanker operations.

Since 2000, Omega Aerial Refuelling Services (OARS) has been the market leader in commercial in-flight refuelling services, having completed more missions and delivered more fuel than any other commercial operator. Their customers include the US military, foreign militaries and US government agencies. With the US Navy, Omega operated under a contract with the Naval Air Systems Command to support US Navy and US Marine Corps flight operations worldwide. They have recently supported deployments of US Navy and USMC aircraft on temporary deployment into Europe as well as into the Gulf region. They have also been actively engaged with the air-to-air refuelling trials of aircraft such as the X-37B UCAV (Unmanned Combat Air Vehicle he F-35 and the CARTS (Conformal Aerial Refuelling Tank System) – a successful collaboration between Lockheed Martin and Cobham to provide a low-cost, high performance probe and drogue aerial refuelling solution for the F-16.

They were also involved in the delivery of F-16F aircraft to the United Emirates Air Force as well as F/A-18 aircraft to the Finnish Air Force and recently supported Exercise Valiant Shield by refuelling eight USMC MV-22B Osprey helicopters of VMM-268 across the Pacific on their long over-water return flight from Darwin, Australia, back to their home at Guam, Hawaii.

OARS operate a US civilian-registered fleet consisting of a K-707 (N707MQ) and a KDC-10 N975VV).

Cherry Air

Another operator in the independent civilian tanker market is Cherry Air, which has purchased the former Royal Australian Air Force (RAAF) C-130A A97-212, which has been registered as N131EC. Despite the aircraft's vintage (having been manufactured back in 1958) it has been fitted with a pair of fourth-generation Cobham 900E wing refuelling pods, each capable of delivering up to 450 US gallons per hour, and is now available for work.

The Drones are Coming

The growth of the drone market and their increased uses in a variety of military fields has required air-to-air refuelling companies such as Cobham to work closely with the designers and operators of Unmanned Aerial Vehicles. Cobham have been at the forefront of testing and developing systems to permit autonomous refuelling from unmanned tanker and receiver drones.

The first time an unmanned aircraft was refuelled in flight occurred during trials on April 2015 in the Atlantic Test Ranges over the Chesapeake Bay when the US Navy's unmanned Northrop-Grumman X-47B UCAV (Unmanned Combat Air Vehicle) took on fuel from an Omega K-707 tanker.

Meanwhile, through its MQ-25 competition, the US Navy created the need for an unmanned refuelling vehicle that would effectively extend the combat range of deployed F/A-18 Super Hornets, EA-18G Growlers and Lockheed Martin F-35C fighters. The unmanned MQ-25 will have to seamlessly integrate with an aircraft carrier's catapult launch and recovery systems.

Initially specified way back in 2006 by the US Navy as the Unmanned Carrier-Launched Airborne Surveillance and Strike (UCLASS) programme, the strike requirements were diluted in order to create an intelligence, surveillance and reconnaissance (ISR)-orientated aircraft that could be developed to conduct counter-terrorism missions in 2012. All that changed again in February 2016; after many delays over the project's priorities, it was reported that a significant portion of the effort would now be aimed at producing a F/A-18E Super Hornet-sized, carrier-based aerial refuelling tanker as the Carrier-Based Aerial-Refuelling System (CBARS), with 'a little ISR', as well as some capabilities for communications relay. Its strike capabilities were delayed until a further version of the vehicle could be developed. In July 2016, it was officially named 'MQ-25 Stingray'.

It is believed that the Pentagon made these significant changes to address the US Navy's expected fighter shortfall by directing funds to buy additional F/A-18E/F Super Hornets and accelerate purchases and development of the F-35C. Having the CBARS system would also free up the current Super Hornet buddy-buddy tanking missions and allow them to operate as originally designed.

On 30 August 2018, it was announced that Boeing will build the first CBARS UAV through an initial $805 million contract to construct, develop and provide four aircraft. The MQ-25 is powered by a Rolls-Royce AE 3007N turbofan engine delivering 10,000 lb (4,500 kg) of static thrust. It is a variant of the engine used to power the US Navy's MQ-4C Triton high-altitude long-endurance UAV.

The MQ-25 Stingray programme is expected to expand up to seventy-two aircraft, potentially worth around $13 billion.

Virtual Refuelling

During the Paris Air Show at Le Bourget in June 2017, Cobham announced a Real-Time Hose and Drogue Dynamic Simulator. Utilising Virtual Reality (VR), the simulator can demonstrate accurate hose-and-drogue behaviour in a synthetic AAR environment.

Basically, it's a virtual reality simulator that offers both training and testing opportunities to its users. Virtual Refuelling uses high fidelity hose and drogue performance models which capture the interaction of all of the components within Cobham's wing pod and centre line systems and can play a significant role in the design of new AAR systems from concept to certification. Any number of different in-flight scenarios or systems can be tested to accurately predict how a system will respond, allowing Cobham to validate and verify new AAR systems before they are built and tested, thereby reducing technology and commercial risks. Currently the potential training opportunities of the virtual reality AAR simulator are being examined, but could prove to be extensive.

With both the KC-135 and KC-10 fleet reaching the end of their lives, the US Air Force was seeking to find a suitable replacement. After a series of bidding processes, the contract was awarded to Boeing for their KC-46A, a derivative of the Boeing 767 airliner. N462KC was photographed undergoing refuelling trials with a US Navy F/A-18 of VX-23, the Strike Test Evaluation Unit, on 11 February 2016. (*US Air Force image via Cobham plc*)

On 24 January 2016, KC-46A N462KC had completed trials with an F-16C from Edwards AFB using the Boeing flying boom. (*US Air Force via Cobham plc*)

On 1 March 2016 N462KC was photographed undergoing refuelling trials with a US Marine Corps AV-8B of VX-31. In addition to the Boeing flying boom, the KC-46A has been configured with a pair of Cobham RP-910E-75 wing-mounted refuelling pods (WARP), and with a Cobham FR-600-84MDR Centreline Drogue System (CDS) located in the rear fuselage. This configuration provides the KC-46A with the flexibility to refuel both large and small aircraft of the US Air Force, US Navy and US Marine Corps. (*US Air Force via Cobham plc*)

Development work with the Airbus A400M Aerial Refuelling System has continued. This example, scheduled for delivery to the Luftwaffe, was photographed on 30 June 2017. (*Airbus Defence and Space*)

An image of Airbus A400M tanker 'EC-404' undergoing trials with a Spanish Air Force EF-18A, serial number C-15-13/12-01, on 11 August 2014. The tanker has a pair of under-wing-mounted Cobham 908E Wing Dispenser Equipment (WDE) units installed. (*Airbus Defence and Space*)

A view approaching the basket of the starboard Cobham 908E WDU. This unit has the potential to dispense up to 400 US gallons per minute. (*Airbus Defence and Space*)

A number of civilian operators have identified a niche in the air-to-air refuelling market, by providing a bespoke system of aerial refuelling services to military operators as and when required – to conduct long-distance delivery flights, for example. One such operator is Omega Aerial Refuelling Services, who operate a Boeing K-707, N707MQ, in addition to this modified DC-10-40, N974VV, seen here refuelling a United Arab Emirates Air Force F-16F, serial number 3003. (*Omega via Cobham plc*)

This image was taken on 18 October 2010 during the flight test programme of the CARTS (Conformal Aerial Refuelling Tank System) – a successful collaboration between Lockheed Martin and Cobham to provide a low-cost, high-performance probe and drogue aerial refuelling solution for the F-16. Interestingly, the refuelling probe telescopically extends and retracts from a purpose-built right-side forward conformal fuel tank. (*Omega via Cobham plc*)

This image, taken on 2 November 2017, shows the Omega Aerial Refuelling Services DC-10 tanker, N974VV, during refuelling trials with an F-35B. As a result of the trials, Omega Aerial Refuelling Services are cleared to provide aerial refuelling services to both F-35B and F-35C Lightning II aircraft. (*Omega Aerial Refuelling Services*)

Cherry Air is another US company who have set themselves up to offer aerial refuelling capabilities to military organisations. They operate the former Royal Australian Air Force (RAAF) C-130A A97-212, which has been registered as N131EC. It was photographed at its home base on 13 December 2010. (*via Cobham plc*)

Despite the aircraft's vintage (having been manufactured back in 1958), it has been fitted with a pair of fourth-generation Cobham 900E wing refuelling pods, each capable of delivering up to 450 US gallons per hour. (*via Cobham plc*)

Working in conjunction with Boeing, Embraer are developing the KC-390, a twin-jet-powered military transport aircraft. In addition to its transport role, Embraer are also developing and testing an aerial refuelling version equipped with a pair of Cobham 912E Wing Refuelling Pods, capable of delivering up to 400 US gallons per side. One of the development aircraft, PT-ZNF, was photographed with both hose units extended. (*Embraer via Cobham plc*)

Helicopters have also benefitted from in-flight refuelling, partly to increase endurance but also to allow the lifting of greater payloads, with a fuel top-up available once the helicopter is in forward flight. This is the view from the flight deck of a Boeing V-22 Osprey while taking on fuel from a US Navy KC-130 from VX-23 based at Patuxent River NAS. (*via Cobham plc*)

Another perspective of the V-22 refuelling from the KC-130. (*via Cobham plc*)

Not satisfied with the MV-22 operating just as an air-to-air receiver, Boeing have been testing the Cobham V-22 Aerial Refuelling System (VARS), which employs a FR300 Hose Drum Unit. MV-22 N204TR (thought to be serial number 165942) was photographed refuelling an F/A-18A from the US Marine Corps' VMFA-314 at Miramar, California. (*via Cobham plc*)

With the proliferation of Unmanned Aerial Vehicles (UAVs) around the world, Cobham is at the forefront of testing and developing systems to permit autonomous refuelling from unmanned tanker and receiver drones. In this image, the tanker, N51457, is registered as a Star Vision Technologies Tanker. (*Cobham plc*)

As far as the US Navy is concerned, the future of air-to-air refuelling clearly lies with the Carrier-Based Aerial-Refuelling System (CBARS). This is Boeing's new MQ-25 Stingray, which is under development to provide refuelling capabilities with the F/A-18E Super Hornet, EA-18G Growler and F-35C fighters. The tanker should be capable of passing 14,000 pounds of fuel to other aircraft at a range of 500 nautical miles from the carrier. (*Boeing*)

The Boeing MQ-25 Stingray CBARS, photographed while completing Deck Handling Demonstrations at St Louis on 26 January 2018. On 30 August 2018, it was announced that Boeing will build the first CBARS UAV through an initial $805 million contract to construct, develop and provide four aircraft. (*Boeing/Eric Shindelbower*)

The shape of AAR in the future? A concept image released by Lockheed Martin shows the new MQ-25 Stingray CBARS in action, refuelling a Lockheed Martin F-35C aircraft. The single refuelling pod is mounted under the centre fuselage of the tanker, although, in reality, the hose length may appear to be a little on the short side? (*Lockheed Martin*)

Bibliography and Sources

Andrews, C. F. and E. B. Morgan, *Vickers Aircraft Since 1908*, Putnam, 2nd edition, 1988.

British Aviation Research Group, *British Military Aircraft Serials and Markings*, British Aviatio
Research Group, 2nd edition, 1983.

Cruddas, Colin, *In Cobham's Company – Sixty Years of Flight Refuelling Limited*, Cobham plc, 199

Flintham, Victor, *Air Wars and Aircraft – A Detailed Record of Air Combat, 1945 to the Prese
Arms and Armour Press, 1989.

Hazell, Steve, *Handley Page Victor* (Warpaint Series No. 36), Warpaint Books Ltd

Hellebrand, Julian, Colin Cruddas, Philip Smart and David Burnett, *Cobham 75*, Cobham plc, 200

Marshall, Sir Arthur, OBE DL, Hon DSC (Cranfield), CRAeS, Hon Fellow Jesus College Cambridg
The Marshall Story – A Century of Wheels and Wings, Patrick Stephens Limited, 1st edition 199

Morgan, Eric B., *Vickers Valiant – The First of the V-Bombers*, Midland Publishing, 2002

Robertson, Bruce, *British Military Aircraft Serials 1878–1987*, Midland Counties Publication
6th edition, 1987.

Tanner, Richard M., *History of Air-to-Air Refuelling*, Pen & Sword Aviation, 2006.

Thetford, Owen, *Aircraft of the Royal Air Force Since 1918*, Putnam, 8th edition, 1988.

Wilson, Keith, *BAC/Vickers VC10 Owners Workshop Manual*, Haynes Publishing, 2016.

Wilson, Keith, *Blackburn/BAE Buccaneer Owners Workshop Manual*, Haynes Publishing, 2018.

Wilson, Keith, *RAF in Camera: 1950s*, Pen & Sword Aviation, 2015.

Wilson, Keith, *RAF in Camera: 1960s*, Pen & Sword Aviation, 2015.

Wilson, Keith, *RAF in Camera: 1970s*, Pen & Sword Aviation, 2017.

Plus the following papers and magazines:

Air-to-Air Refuelling Methods, Flight Refuelling Limited, 1997.

Vickers B9/48 Jet Bomber Range, Bomb Load Performance, Unrefuelled and Flight Refuelled, Flig
Refuelling, 1951.

Various issues of *The Aeroplane*, *Flight* and *Flight International* magazines.